YOU ARE AN ABUNDANT B

YOU ARE AN abundant B

THE **NO BS GUIDE** TO MANIFESTING

AUDREY FAUST, THE MANIFESTING CFO™

DISCLAIMER

This book is intended for educational and inspirational purposes only. While the author shares tools, strategies, and perspectives related to money, mindset, and personal growth, nothing in this book should be considered financial, legal, tax, medical, or mental health advice.

The author is not acting as a licensed therapist, financial advisor, or other professional provider. If you are struggling with your mental health, experiencing distress, or need personalized guidance, please seek support from a qualified professional.

Any income, transformation, or success stories referenced are examples and are not promises or guarantees. Results vary from person to person. You are responsible for your choices, actions, and outcomes, and the author and publisher disclaim any liability for your use of the information contained in this book.

All names referenced in this book have been changed for confidentiality

"YOU BECOME WHAT YOU BELIEVE. AND TO BELIEVE THAT YOU ARE CREATED BY A POWER GREATER THAN YOURSELF MEANS ANYTHING IS POSSIBLE."

—OPRAH WINFREY

CONTENTS

READY TO STOP SETTLING FOR "JUST ENOUGH" AND START LIVING IN OVERFLOW?

For too long, women entrepreneurs have been told to work harder, stay small, and be grateful for scraps. It's time to stop apologizing for wanting more and start remembering who the hell you are.

In *You Are an Abundant B*, self-made multi-millionaire, and Manifesting CFO™ Audrey Faust shares the truth and exact steps to manifesting money, because it isn't just magic, it's actual brain science too.

Through raw personal stories, powerful client transformations, and the exact tools she uses to help women grow profitable businesses, Audrey shows you how to rewire your beliefs, shift your energy, and become a magnet for money.

You'll learn:

- How to change your brain in order to change your bank account
- Audrey's signature Dishing the T.E.A. Framework: Thoughts, Energy, Alignment
- How to tap, visualize, and prime your brain for the financial success you deserve
- Her secret client tools and 70-Day Money Manifestation Activation to reprogram your reality for abundance

It's your practical-meets-magical guide to manifesting money, living in overflow, and stepping into your role as the powerful, abundant female business owner you were meant to be, because moneymoney responds to energy. And your energy is everything.
And your energy is everything.

This book is an invitation to believe bigger, because the moment you do, the universe rises to meet you.

part one

AWAKENING TO ABUNDANCE

chapter one

THE DAY I STOPPED PLAYING SMALL AND BECAME THE MANIFESTING CFO

Dear Abundant B,

Let's talk about the shitty beliefs keeping you broke and scared. We'll cut right to it. You weren't born to play small, scrape by, or hustle your way into worthiness. You were born for wealth, overflow, and a life so aligned it turns heads. But somewhere along the way, maybe between childhood conditioning, money drama, and a million quiet moments of self-doubt, you might have forgotten.

And just so we're clear, Abundant B isn't just a cute name. It's who you are. B stands for Boss. Bestie. Badass. Babe. Beauty. Bold. Brilliant. Buttercup. Bitch (in the best, unapologetic way). Fill in your own B-word, because this is about you claiming all the versions of you you've been told to dim down.

This book is your wake-up call. It's your time to step into your own power.

You've been told to budget harder, manifest more, or just "think positive." But no one said to you that your beliefs were running the show. That the invisible thoughts swirling in your mind, about money, success, safety, and self-worth, are actually what is shaping your reality. And Abundant B, bottom line, if you want to change your bank account, you've got to change your brain.

You don't need another spreadsheet. You need a shift. An energetic, unshakeable, soul-deep upgrade that turns you into the woman who knows she's abundant because she decided to be.

I've been there. Stuck, scared, and questioning if I had what it took. This isn't just a book about making more money. It's about remembering who the hell you are, Ms. Abundant B.

If you want to grab all the fabulous tools and links I'm going to share with you, here is the QR code for my free book portal with all the goodies.

Now, before we dive into all the tools, the tapping, money magic, and the manifestation, I want to take you back in time a little, back to the girl who hadn't yet remembered how powerful she was.

Let's get one thing straight: Your childhood programming isn't your fault, but it sure as hell is your responsibility now. Most of the beliefs we carry come from childhood.

My earliest childhood belief is that I was stupid. I believed I was stupid because my brother constantly told me so. I didn't have the best brother. He continually belittled me, and I started to think I was inferior. I know his cutting remarks stemmed from his own insecurity. However, I looked up to him and took what he said as truth. And no one ever corrected him. In fact, I think my mother believed it too. It's hard to come back from that. I also found evidence that it was true. I struggled in school and never felt like I was smart. I believed I simply wasn't cut out to be one of the smart ones.

That belief shaped my entire life, my reality, and my energy. It prevented me from seeing my worth and made me feel small, like I was carrying a weight vest I couldn't take off.

For years, that "I'm stupid" story dictated every decision I made, what risks I took, what I asked for, and what I believed I could have. I dimmed myself before life ever had the chance to say no.

Too scared to take the SATs, because of this belief, I took what felt like the safest route. Instead of going to college, I entered a one-year business school program. It was my first small step toward proving to myself that maybe I wasn't as broken as I thought. I worked hard, did well, and for the first time thought, maybe I can actually do this.

Fast-forward a few years, I got married, had two kids before 30, and found myself balancing diapers and debt. I did taxes at night while raising babies by day. Accounting felt easy, finally, something that made sense.

One day, while doing my own tax return, I realized we qualified for government assistance. The shame I felt hit me like a brick to the chest. How the hell did I end up here? That single moment of embarrassment became the spark that lit everything that came next.

I could still hear my brother's voice saying, "You're stupid," in my head. That was the moment I decided to prove him wrong, not through perfection, but through persistence. My kids deserved choices, and so did I.

So, at 30, I enrolled in college to study accounting. That decision changed my entire life. I picked up night shifts, studied when the kids slept, and little by little, the woman who once believed she was stupid started to see new evidence. I realized I could work hard, and when I did, I could figure things out.

That belief became my new north star. It carried me through every exam, every long night, every moment I doubted myself. After a few accounting courses under my belt, I started my own accounting business so I could be there for my kids and still grow something of my own. That business gave me flexibility, confidence, and proof that I could create success on my own terms.

I didn't know it then, but I was already reprogramming my brain, teaching it that I wasn't stupid. I was capable if I worked hard enough.

I had no clue that this choice would eventually lead me to running multiple businesses, becoming a CFO, and coaching women on money mindset and building wealth. But the Universe always knew, of course she did!

With this new belief guiding me, my business continued to grow. I spent the next several years helping multi-six-and-seven-figure businesses expand, managing millions in revenue, and becoming known as the go-to CFO for growth-minded leaders.

I loved helping clients grow their businesses and planned for and managed every financial and business detail to ensure no unwelcome surprises. But beneath the success, there was still a hum of anxiety, and I was terrified that if I let go of complete control, things would fall apart. Still, I knew that to keep growing, I had to hire a team.

Working with a mindset coach, I did the hard work of reframing my thoughts and challenging my old beliefs about control and my worth. She helped me see that all my success had been fueled by fear—fear of failing, fear of losing control, fear of not being enough. Once I released that, everything expanded with less effort.

Still, there was a whisper in my soul saying, "There's more than this."

As I worked with more clients, I began to notice a pattern. No matter their revenue, every business owner I supported eventually hit the same wall—their mindset. The very beliefs that once held me back were holding them back too. That realization lit a fire in me. I knew numbers alone couldn't fix what was rooted inside their own beliefs.

So in 2021, I followed that whisper and enrolled in a NeuroCoaching certification program because I wanted to help my clients reprogram the beliefs that were keeping them stuck around money, success, and enoughness.

The program focused on reprogramming subconscious beliefs—those thought loops that quietly run the show. As I brought what I learned into my work, my clients started experiencing massive mindset shifts, and their results followed.

That moment, though I didn't know it, would be the bridge between two worlds the strategy of business and the psychology of success. It was the spark that set my evolution in motion, leading to what would soon become "The Manifesting CFO."

Not long after I began blending mindset work into my financial coaching, two of my largest CFO clients announced they were selling their companies. Of course, that was the goal we'd been working toward, and I was thrilled for them. But it also meant I was about to lose multi-six figures of my company's revenue in one fell swoop.

I remember sitting on a call, coaching one of these clients through his nerves about accepting a life-changing offer. I laughed afterward, realizing I had just coached myself out of my largest client and over 60% of my revenue.

The deals took a couple of months to finalize, and during that time, I found myself staring at the blank space that comes before a new beginning. It felt like the Universe had cleared my schedule on purpose, but stepping into the "unknown" terrified me. It wasn't just a normal uncertainty; it was a deep, physical fear that at that moment..

Around the same time, my team member decided to leave accounting to pursue her own dream. Another sign. The Universe wasn't being subtle; it was time to leap.

When one of my departing clients offered to keep me on after their acquisition, my entire body said no. That sinking feeling told me everything I needed to know. It was time to trust the pull.

Even though we had plenty of savings to hold us over financially, I had a huge knot in my stomach that wouldn't go away. The Universe was pointing me in this direction, but I was scared out of my mind. So I decided it was time to bring out my secret tool belt, the one my CFO clients never knew I had. The part of me that trusted intuition, energy, and the unseen. The "woo." I'd kept it quiet for years, but now it was time to let it lead and show the world.

If you're new to that term, "woo" is what I call the mystical, intuitive side of success, the part that reminds us we're guided, supported, and never alone. And if your logical mind wants to roll its eyes, good. That's exactly how mine felt at first.

So I started with an Akashic reading from my colleague, Carissa. I didn't know exactly what I was looking for, only that I needed clarity. What came through in that session changed everything.

Carissa confirmed I was being guided toward a new path. I asked, "So why isn't it happening faster?" She smiled and said, "There are things you still need to learn, tools to master, and beliefs to release. But it won't take as long as you think. Once you discover those tools, your path will start revealing itself." Her words gave me peace and confirmation that I was being guided. I tucked them away and said to myself, "Okay, Universe, I'm listening."

A few weeks later, another colleague whom I admired and respected, Carol, invited me to a group tapping session. I'd seen people do tapping before and honestly thought it looked a little ridiculous. But something in me said, "Go." So I did.

Tapping is a simple yet powerful technique in which you gently tap specific points on your face and body while acknowledging what you're feeling. It helps calm the nervous system, release emotional blocks, and rewire subconscious beliefs.

I volunteered for what's called a tapping seat and shared my fear of the unknown. Logically, I knew we were fine financially, but my body was still screaming that we weren't safe. Carol asked a few gentle questions, and we uncovered what was hiding underneath: a deep-rooted belief that the "unknown" wasn't safe.

It all went back to my childhood. My dad had bipolar disorder, and when he went into manic episodes, my mom would send us to our rooms. Most of the time, he was loving and kind, but when he was manic, he'd yell and throw things. He never hurt us physically, but emotionally, the unpredictability left its mark. It taught me that the unknown was dangerous.

Suddenly, everything made sense. That was why I'd clung to control, why I over-planned, why I held on to clients like a life raft. Of course, I feared letting go. The unknown had never felt safe before.

So we tapped through it all. I felt the energy shift from my stomach down through my legs and out of my hands. It was the strangest, most freeing feeling I'd ever experienced.

I tapped on the fear of the unknown every day for a few days, and then one morning, it hit me. I wasn't afraid anymore. Not even a little. In fact, I felt excited about what was coming. The fear that had once ruled my life was gone, just like that. I knew, deep in my bones, that I was safe. That magic of tapping blew me away.

People talk about financial freedom. But this? This was freedom from my thoughts. This was the kind of freedom that comes from knowing the Universe has your back, that you don't have to be afraid of the unknown anymore.

I was so moved by the transformation that I became a certified tapping practitioner and began weaving it into my work with women. Because here's the truth I saw every damn day as a coach: There's so much emotion tied to money, and most of it runs quietly in the background in our subconscious. And when I remembered what Carissa had said about learning new tools, I knew this was one of them.

And what happened next was even more powerful. I said to myself, "Let's start manifesting money like a badass." Not through hustle, but through high-vibe energy, alignment, and hours and hours of belief reprogramming. So I immersed myself in books, courses, meditation, music, journaling, and future pulling. I started noticing the common threads. I also noticed where I'd been blocking myself. And now, with space in my schedule and the freedom to explore, I committed to going all in.

Two and a half weeks into this immersion, the Universe dropped the mic.

I manifested $29,000.

Yes, really. How? I'll break it all down in the chapters that follow. But let's just say, my mind was officially blown.

I had never been able to manifest like this before, or so I thought. But when I looked back, I realized I'd been manifesting things all along. Never this much money at once, but I'd manifested my husband, several homes, jobs, my business, and my lifestyle.

All of those started as a thought or a dream, and step by step, those thoughts became my reality. Some came with tiny actions, some with big leaps, but all of them were manifestations.

I was a brave, mighty manifesting maven. I simply hadn't realized it. And you, Abundant B, probably haven't either.

After manifesting the $29,000, I decided to keep going all in for a few months to see what else was possible. If the results kept flowing (and honestly, I had no doubt they would), I would start a group program for women. Something that blended all of it, mindset, manifestation, and energy work with my financial expertise. This was too powerful to keep to myself.

Watching other women rise into their wealth and grow their businesses has always lit me up because when a woman feels safe to hold more money, visibility, and power, everything changes for her, her family, her clients, and her legacy.

When I told two of my business besties, Lily and Hailey, what I was doing, they both said, "I want in."

That's when I knew these ideas weren't just something that would work for me. My experiences activated something powerful that other women wanted to experience too. My story wasn't just landing with my besties; it was lighting them up from the inside out.

I was thrilled. Not only would they get to experience the shifts for themselves, but I'd also get proof that this process could work for others, too.

And oh, did it ever. Lily, a leadership coach, tripled her revenue in just a few weeks by shifting her beliefs and energy around money. She showed up differently. She became more confident and stopped questioning herself. That power rapidly showed up in her income.

Hailey, a creative entrepreneur who had always felt a bit disconnected from money, finally saw that her energy around money mattered. She started doing the daily mindset work, tapping, visualizing, and figuring out offers that really ignited excitement in her. She stopped telling herself stories about being "bad with money" or "my clients won't pay for that" and started making powerful, aligned financial decisions. Her confidence skyrocketed, and so did her sales.

Their success cracked me wide open.

This wasn't just personal anymore; it was a purpose!

And I couldn't wait to bring it to more women.

That's how the Money Mindset and Manifestation Accelerator was born—a community where women come together to rise. And Hailey and Lily were my first two members.

Looking back now, that was the day I stopped playing small, not just in business, but in how I saw myself. The woman who once dimmed her light to feel safe was gone. I had finally remembered who I was meant to be all along, the Manifesting CFO, fully in her power.

I blended everything I knew about money, mindset, and subconscious rewiring I had been working on for years. I brought in the energy work, EFT tapping, intuitive practices, and alignment to create a space where women could release old money stories, reset their nervous systems, and receive more than they ever thought possible.

It all brought me back to that Akashic reading I had with Carissa, where she told me I was being guided to something new I hadn't fully uncovered yet. That I had to learn a few more tools and shift a few more beliefs before the full path would be revealed.

I had never felt more aligned or more excited. This was the path. And the tools? They weren't just for me. They were meant to be shared.

What began as a personal transformation quickly became a ripple effect, reaching women who were ready to change their relationship with money, step into abundance, and finally feel safe holding more wealth without hustle or burnout and with alignment, energy, and clarity.

This wasn't just about teaching women how to make more money. It was about helping them remember who they really are, an Abundant B, and what they're capable of.

You, Abundant B, were born for overflow, ease, and wealth that feels aligned at the soul level. It's time to reclaim your throne, release old beliefs that have kept you stuck, and shift your energy to activate unshakable confidence in yourself. You get to step into your power and create lasting wealth fully. You were born to be rich. Now it's time to claim it. And that's exactly what this book will help you do.

Welcome to your next level, Abundant B!

The fact that you're holding this book right now is no accident. You were guided here. Something inside you already knows you were meant for more, and this book is proof.

Let me be clear. This isn't just another book you read once and set aside. This is an experience—a living, breathing portal into your next level of abundance. I can't wait to see you on the other side!

Think of this book as a workbook, a journal, a coaching session, and a mirror all wrapped into one. You didn't come here just to learn about abundance. You came here to embody it.

Each chapter is woven with stories, truths, and practices designed to move you from thinking about abundance to actually living it. You'll notice that the chapters are interactive. You'll find prompts to guide your reflection and journaling, visualizations to activate your imagination and align your energy, tapping scripts to release subconscious blocks and rewire your beliefs, and mantras to anchor you into your new identity. I've seen women shift so profoundly in my workshops that they were moved to tears. That's the kind of transformation waiting for you in these pages. Not simply information, but real breakthroughs. You'll hear some amazing stories from clients. Please note: all client names have been changed to protect their confidentiality.

In Part 1, Awakening to Abundance, you'll discover the truth about women and wealth, and the powerful conditioning that holds us back. In Part 2, you'll learn my signature framework, Dishing the T-E-A—Thoughts, Energy, and Alignment—the three ingredients that will change the way you create everything in your life. In Part 3, Creating Abundance, you'll step into the tools and practices that blend financial strategy with spiritual power so you can truly live as an Abundant B. And in Part Four, you'll experience the 70-Day Money Manifestation Activation, a daily practice that will anchor this work into your bones.

And because I want you to feel this work in every cell of your body, be sure to go into the Book Portal I created just for you. I mentioned this earlier in this chapter, but I'm repeating it because I don't want you to miss out. Inside, you'll find audio versions of the visualizations so you can close your eyes and let yourself be guided. You'll find a video example of tapping so you can watch me demonstrate exactly how to use this powerful tool. And you'll find a workbook for the 70-Day Money Manifestation Activation, giving you space to reflect, journal, and put these practices into action every day. And so much more!

So before you get started, sign up here for the Book Portal–It's 100% free for you because you bought this book.

There may be things in these chapters that shock you, things you question at first, or things you've heard before but never in this way. That's precisely why I wrote this book. I've studied money mindset and manifesting for years, but I never found a book that explained it in a way that was both magical and practical, clear enough to actually use in daily life. I wanted to create the book I always wished I had. A book that doesn't just inspire you for a moment, but gives you fundamental tools you can return to again and again.

Here's my invitation. Don't just skim these pages. Live them. Highlight the lines that stir something in you. Pause when you reach a prompt and actually write it out. Say the mantras out loud until you feel them vibrate through your body. Tap through the scripts and notice how quickly your energy shifts. Listen to the audio, watch the video, and use the workbook. The more you engage with this book, the more it will engage with you.

And please, reach out to me! I love hearing how this book has shifted your thinking, helped you take bold steps, or created new wins in your life and business. Find me on the social platform you love most and tag me in your "Aha" moments and victories. That is why I wrote this book, because your breakthroughs light me up.

And if you love what you're experiencing here, consider sharing this book with a friend or even starting a small book club. Abundance is even more powerful when you experience it in a community, and you'll be amazed at the conversations, support, and breakthroughs that come when women walk through this work together.

If you want to go even deeper, I'd love to invite you into my Money Mindset and Manifestation Accelerator. That's where women gather to practice these tools in real time, celebrate wins, clear blocks together, and hold space for each other's next level. Whether it's with your own circle or by joining mine, know this: Your energy multiplies when you manifest in a group. There's something magical about doing this work together. The breakthroughs come faster, and the celebrations are so much sweeter.

By the time you finish, you won't just have information, you'll have transformation. You'll have a lived experience of abundance. You'll have practiced new ways of thinking, shifted your energy, and stepped into the identity of the Abundant B version of you who creates wealth with ease, joy, and confidence.

Take a deep breath. Exhale. Smile. You're about to unlock the wealthiest, most abundant version of yourself. Are you ready? Good. Let's begin. Cheers to your success!

chapter Two

SEVEN ASTONISHING TRUTHS ABOUT WOMEN, WEALTH & WORTH

While I love tapping, vision boards, and spiritual guidance, nothing woke me up faster than when I heard this statistic: According to a 2024 Wells Fargo report , 90% of women-owned businesses make less than $50,000 a year.

As a CFO, I see numbers all the time, but this hit me differently. I thought, how are so many brilliant, hardworking women earning so little? I remember telling my book writing coach, Sara, "Hell no, I need to do something about this." And that is how this book was born. At that moment, I decided to be an exception and start my own journey to becoming a seven-figure earner too. Because I knew, if I could do it, you could too.

I don't share the stats in this chapter to scare you. They're here to free you, as they did me. Because once you know what you're up against, you get to choose differently. These truths will probably piss you off. I know they did me.

These statistics are the result of conditioning, silence, shame, and outdated beliefs about worth, wealth, and success. Truth is power, and once you know them, you can't unknow them. You get to do something about them. You get to rise and help other women entrepreneurs do the same. Once one woman rises, she opens a door for ten more.

This is why I write, why I speak, and why I coach. Because you weren't born to play small or apologize for wanting more, you were born to be a rich, Abundant B. Let's start to rewrite the rules and rise. Together, we'll open more doors and change these numbers.

TRUTH #1: 90% OF WOMEN-OWNED BUSINESSES MAKE LESS THAN $50,000 A YEAR

Nearly nine out of 10 women-owned businesses without employees earn less than $50,000 per year.

Let that sink in. That is the fire that lit my ass up to write this book. That means nine out of ten women who start a business are barely scraping by. They are earning less than what many full-time jobs pay. For all the risk, responsibility, and hustle? WTF! Most are stuck in survival mode.

And here's the kicker. It's not because we aren't smart or hard-working. It's because we've been conditioned to play small due to some deeply ingrained belief that is holding us back.

We undercharge. We overdeliver. We call it a "side hustle" or tell ourselves, "I'm not in it for the money." But deep down, we want more. And we should, damn it! We deserve more! You didn't come here to make scraps. You get to build wealth. You get to create freedom. You get to leave a legacy.

And that starts with dropping the lie that wanting more makes you greedy, selfish, or too much. Or it's not good or "lady-like" to want more. Or "I should be happy with what I have."

Pick your poison. Whatever story keeps you small. It's time to let it go of it, beautiful.

Abundant B Reframe:

> I'm not here to play small. I'm here to play big, profit big, and I give myself full permission to rise.

TRUTH #2: ONLY 1.7% OF WOMEN-OWNED BUSINESSES EVER HIT 7 FIGURES

According to a 2025 Forbes article, only 1.7% of U.S. women-owned businesses ever generate $1 million or more in annual revenue.

Let's just call this what it is: unacceptable. Less than 2%. That means out of every 100 women who start a business, only one or two ever cross the million-dollar mark. This breaks my heart. Why? I know it's not for lack of talent or drive. It's not because we aren't capable. It's because we've been taught to dream small, charge less, and settle for "good enough."

And honestly? I was one of them. I stayed stuck under the ceiling for way too long because I didn't know how to think like a powerful woman. I knew how to hustle, and boy, did I. I knew how to work hard. But I didn't know how to expand. I didn't really truly own my worth or value. And I sure as hell didn't know how to receive it.

Here's what I've learned. Hitting seven figures is not reserved for the lucky, the flashy, or the chosen few. The ones who somehow have a magic secret that no one else has. It's available to every single woman who's willing to shift her beliefs, own her worth, and lead like an Abundant B she was born to be.

That's why this book isn't about just making more money. It's about becoming the woman who no longer flinches at a million-dollar goal. The woman who attracts, not chases. Who is powerful, grounded, and loving. Who knows she is worth it and is willing to invest in herself like she means it. Who claims her abundance because she was made for it. This is the Abundant B.

Abundant B Reframe:

> I'm not the exception. I'm the example. I get to grow a million-dollar business and do it in a way that feels aligned, empowered, and 100% true to me.

TRUTH #3: WOMEN UNDERCHARGE BY 28%

According to the Women's Small Business Report by FreshBooks, women entrepreneurs charge, on average, 28% less than men for the same services.

No wonder so many of us are not profitable. We talk about the corporate gender pay gap, but when it comes to our own business? This one is 100% on us. We are setting our own prices. We are setting the bar. And on top of that, we constantly second-guess ourselves, worry that no one will buy, and question our value and worth.

Here is the truth: We are brilliant, powerful, kick-ass women. We work hard and give it our all every damn day. We deserve to earn as much as, or even more than men.

So why do we constantly undervalue ourselves and second-guess our pricing?

We were taught to play small. We were taught not to "outshine" our male counterparts. We were taught to "be happy with what we have." We also believe that charging more might be "greedy," "selfish," or "ungrateful."

That's total bullshit—all of it.

We deserve to earn as much as, or even more than, our male counterparts doing the same work. You bring brilliance, strategy, and soul to your work. You get results. Let your pricing reflect that. It's time to level up, buttercup, starting today.

Abundant B Reframe:

I price with power. I don't discount my brilliance. I charge in full alignment with the transformation
I create, and I let money meet me there.

TRUTH #4: OVER HALF OF BUSINESS OWNERS FLY BLIND

Here are two stats that make my CFO heart hurt:

According to PR Newswire, 56% of small business owners make decisions with outdated or incomplete financial data. And QuickBooks reports that 60% of business owners say they aren't confident in their accounting or finance knowledge.

Honestly? I see it all the damn time. They often wonder why they're not profitable.

They wonder why cash flow is always tight. They wonder why it feels like they're working so hard and barely seeing any reward.

More often than not, the answer is right there in their financials. I can spot it in minutes.

The problem is that their books are not up to date. Or if they are, they're just not looking. Or they might not understand what to look at because no one taught them.

They are making decisions 100% based on emotion rather than on data. They wonder why they're not profitable, stressed with no cash, and thinking about throwing in the towel.

Let me be straight with you. Every answer you're looking for is sitting inside your monthly financial reports. But if your books aren't up to date, and you're not reviewing them consistently every month, you're flying blind.

Here's what you can do to change this. Keep your books current every single month. Review your Profit & Loss, Balance Sheet, and Cash Flow Statement. Use that data to make powerful, informed decisions. Every month. Yes, every month. Because if you wait until the end of the year, the story is over. The story could be a fairytale or a nightmare, but you can't change the story if you're not reading and writing it along the way.

Now, I get it, trust me. You might not understand these reports (yet). You might even feel afraid to look. So many women are. Put on your big girl pants and let's get started because courage creates confidence and confidence brings clarity. Avoiding your numbers won't get you anywhere. But facing them, that's where the magic happens.

I know you were never taught this. That's why I'm here.

Abundant B Reframe:

> I don't avoid my numbers. I own them. I use my financial reports to lead, grow, and profit like a true Abundant B CEO.

TRUTH #5: WOMEN STRUGGLE TO RECEIVE

Let's talk about receiving for a minute. I see this every day with my clients. So many women wait until they're overwhelmed, burned out, or ready to give up before they finally ask for support, because they've been conditioned to believe they should be able to do it all on their own.

As women, we are so damn used to giving, we find it very difficult to receive. It's possible it's built into our DNA. As mothers, we need to be givers. That's a very demanding job. And a lot of women were never taught to be able to receive. Again, back to the conditioning that says women should not want more, should be the nurturer, should be the giver of all givers. Well, I'm done with the "shoulds." It's time we stop "shoulding" all over ourselves. There are no "shoulds." Let's replace them with "get to." Let's empower ourselves and decide what we truly want and "get to" have, versus what we "should" do, "should" have, or "should" be grateful for. We deserve more.

We get to ask for help. We get to receive help. We get to be cared for, too. If you are serving from an empty cup, how about trying to fill it back up and serve from the overflow? That is when we can thrive. That is when we can become the most Abundant B you've ever seen. That is how we get to show up in the world.

I see this in my clients all the time. They wait until everything is a mess and they are ready to give up. They are so overwhelmed because they think they can do it all. Bring home the bacon and fry it up in a pan. Isn't that how the song goes? Because we were taught that needing help is weak. And if we are strong, we "shouldn't" need help. We can do it all ourselves. We'll do it better anyway. We think that needing help means we're not good enough, smart enough, or capable enough.

The truth is, receiving isn't weak. It's standing in your Abundant B feminine power.

And creating abundance and manifesting is all about receiving. You have to practice receiving if you want to bring the abundance in. If you can't receive, you won't attract, and you will deflect abundance.

Start saying "yes" to help. Start asking for help. Start stepping into your Abundant B power so you can receive all the abundance that is due to you now. You've already worked hard. You've already busted your ass. Now it's time to receive. Now is your time to shine. You don't have to work harder. You just have to let it come in.

Abundant B Reframe:

> I don't have to do it all alone. I open myself to receive support, wealth, and abundance because I'm worthy of it.

TRUTH #6: WOMEN EQUATE WORKING HARDER WITH EARNING MORE

Let's talk about working harder. According to a SCORE study, 33% of small business owners report working more than 50 hours per week, and 25% work more than 60 hours.

Women are probably the majority of that statistic. I see it every day. So many women wear hard work like a badge of honor. If we hustle more, grind more, give more, the money will finally come. Or will it?

Here's the thing: remember Truth #1: 90% of women-owned businesses make less than $50,000 a year. Do the math with me: If you're working 50 hours a week (which, let's be real, most women entrepreneurs are), that breaks down to $19.23 an hour. That's barely more than the minimum wage in some places. And that's for running a business. Carrying the risk, maybe even managing a team, doing all the things, including the mental exhaustion when you lie awake at night wondering how you are going to pay for everything. I see you.

Meanwhile, the men aren't necessarily working harder; they're just charging more, receiving more, and believing they're worth more.

Here's the truth: working harder does not equal earning more. Often it equals earning less. Earning more comes from alignment. From belief. From owning your value. From shifting the inside before expecting a different result on the outside.

When you keep tying your income to your effort, you trap yourself in the soul-sucking, time-for-money hamster wheel, even if you "work for yourself." Let's break that cycle, shall we?

Abundant B Reframe:

> I no longer trade time for worth. I receive more by owning my value, not by overworking for it. I set boundaries.

TRUTH #7: SUCCESS TRIGGERS FEAR

Oh boy, do we know this word well. I'm sure you've heard the acronyms: Forget Everything And Run or Face Everything And Rise. As Abundant Bs, we Rise, we don't Run. But our DNA is wired for fear, automatically. In caveman (and cavewoman) days, our brains were programmed for survival, which meant "run." Survival also meant fitting in, not standing out. So what happens now when we see success and visibility? When we step into our power to be seen? Our subconscious goes haywire and says, "Retreat," Run," Danger," "Hide."

We've also been conditioned that we aren't "allowed" to be successful or to "win." That we have to dim our light and play small, pull back instead of rising when things start to take off.

Why? Because we weren't taught we could win. We weren't taught that we were allowed to rise higher than the men in the room. We were taught to support, not shine. We were taught to assist, not be ambitious.

Even though the world has changed (thank God), our subconscious beliefs have not yet caught up. We get to start to change that. Right here, right now. We get to break the generational patterns. We get to rewire our relationship with success and winning. Because we no longer have to run when fear knocks on our door. Abundant Bs rise and expand when fear comes to the door.

Abundant B Reframe:

> I am safe to rise. I no longer run from success. I welcome it, embody it, and let it expand me into the woman I was born to be.

These truths are a wake-up call. You don't need fixing. You're not broken. And you're certainly not behind, you're just becoming. You've just been handed beliefs that were never yours to begin with. But now that you see them clearly, you get to choose differently.

These statistics don't define you. They do invite you to rise. To say yes to your next level, even if it feels scary. You get to take ownership of your business, your money, your energy, and your future. We don't change these numbers by waiting, by playing small, by being invisible. We change them by becoming the woman who decides. The woman who rises and says, "I'm done playing small. I'm ready for more."

Every time you raise your prices, say yes to support, look at your numbers, become more visible, or claim your space, you are taking a stand not just for yourself, but for every woman watching, for your sisters, your daughters, and all future generations of women. When one woman rises, it creates massive momentum. It shows other women what is possible. That's how we shift this conversation. That's how we build real wealth. One courageous step at a time.

What's holding you back isn't outside of you. It's your thoughts and subconscious beliefs that more often than not, you are unaware of. And in the next chapter, we're going to start discovering them. You'll see exactly how your thoughts and beliefs are still shaping your results and your future, and exactly how to release them for good so you can rise.

You don't have to live on autopilot anymore. You don't have to wait for rock bottom, burnout, or the next breakdown to shift. You get to begin now. You get to turn the page. Because you are an Abundant B. And this is just the beginning, beautiful Abundant B.

So let's keep going.

"DISHING THE T-E-A" FRAMEWORK

chapter three

THE "T" IN TEA: FLIP THE THOUGHTS THAT ATTRACT ABUNDANCE

Abundant B, get ready, because in the following three chapters, we're going to be Dishing the T-E-A.

Not the gossip kind (although, if you've got stories, I'm here for them), but the kind that actually changes your life: Thoughts, Energy, and Alignment.

These are the three key ingredients to manifestation and attracting abundance. And just like a perfect recipe, if even one of them is off, the end result is, well, meh. But when you get them all working together? That's when life gets delicious.

In this chapter, we're starting with the "T"—Thoughts—because everything begins here. Your thoughts are the starting point for every single thing you've ever created, good or bad. They're the secret designers of your reality, quietly shaping the way you feel, the actions you take, and ultimately, the results you get.

So, let's start pouring the tea on the thoughts running your life. And I'm not talking about the cute, Pinterest-worthy affirmations you write in your journal. I mean the gritty, unfiltered beliefs whispering in the background, shaping your reality when you're not even paying attention.

I didn't know it at the time, but for decades, mine sounded like this: "You're not smart enough."

"You have to work harder than everyone else just to keep up."

"Don't trust anyone else with your work. They'll just screw it up."

"Six figures is great. Don't get greedy."

I thought these statements were facts. Hardwired truths about who I was and how the world worked. I didn't realize they were just thoughts, beliefs, and subconscious programming. It wasn't until my late 40s that I found out I could actually change them. And honestly, Abundant B, my mind was blown.

By the time I hired my first mindset coach, I had clawed my way to six figures in my accounting business. It had taken grit, late nights, weekends, and sheer willpower, and more diet soda than I'd like to admit. I had hustled myself to the bone and wore it like a badge of honor. Because somewhere deep down, I believed I wasn't smart enough to get ahead on genius alone, so I had to outwork everyone else. That's what I did in college, in corporate, and in my business. That is what got me through. If I just pushed harder than the next person, I'd make it, I'd succeed.

But there was no more "harder" left in me. I was at capacity. Maxed out. I was stuck in my own loop: work harder, burn out, keep control, stay small.

I told myself I should be happy with my six-figure business. I mean, wasn't that the dream? I could pay my bills, take vacations, and buy the shoes. But that was my ego talking. And your ego,

Abundant B, is sneaky as hell. It will disguise fear as "practicality." It will tell you to "be realistic" when you're standing on the edge of your next big breakthrough. It will whisper, "You're fine where you are," but what it really means is, "Don't you dare grow, because growth means change, and change feels unsafe."

When I started working with my mindset coach, she asked me questions no one had ever asked me before.

When did this belief first show up in your life?

Where did you learn that hard work is the only way to succeed? What about working smarter?

Why do you believe it's all about hard work?

It felt like she was poking holes in the foundation of my entire life.

There were many actual tears shed in and out of the session. Every tear was the beginning of a transformational breakthrough. I didn't realize it then, but I know it now. Every time I am coaching someone on money mindset and the tears creep in, I know we've landed on the belief that has been holding them back, keeping them small for way too long.

All those thoughts running my business weren't facts. They were beliefs. And beliefs can be changed.

Once I started shifting those core beliefs, my entire business changed. I went from a solo six-figure grind to a multi–six–figure CFO consulting agency. I built a team. We served multi–seven–figure clients. We had systems, and I had breathing room.

And it wasn't because I suddenly learned some secret accounting hack. It was because I became a different woman, the one who made different decisions because she believed different things.

I stopped seeing my thoughts as unchangeable. I started seeing them for what they were, the starting point of everything. It's worth repeating: Your thoughts are not just passing fluff in your head. They are the invisible creators of your life. They spark your emotions. Your emotions drive your actions. And your actions, or your inactions, create your results.

And that sequence is what I like to call the TEAR model: Thoughts → Emotions → Actions → Results.

Have you ever felt like you're doing everything right? You're showing up, taking action, visualizing, journaling, and yet it still feels like something invisible is holding you back.

That's exactly what happened for Dianne, one of the women inside my Money Mindset and Manifestation Accelerator. She looked up at me during a session and said, "I feel like I have one foot on the gas and one foot on the brake."

The room went quiet. Every woman there nodded, because they had felt it too. That frustrating push-pull between wanting more and somehow slowing yourself down just as things start to pick up.

When I asked her to fill in the blank, "Rich people are ___________," without thinking she said, "Selfish."

Then she quickly added, "Oh, but I don't believe that."

And consciously, she didn't. But, Abundant B, when I ask a question like that, the first word that pops out of your mind, before you can edit or justify it, is usually the truth your subconscious is running. Most of us skip over that first word and go searching for the "right" or more socially acceptable answer. But that first response? That's the one quietly shaping your emotions, actions, and results.

Dianne's answer revealed what was happening beneath the surface. Her conscious mind wanted more abundance, but her subconscious was still running an old story: Rich people are selfish.

Somewhere along the way, Dianne had absorbed messages like:

"You have enough."

"People with money are selfish."

Her subconscious heard those words and translated them into a rule: It's not safe to want more.

This pattern showed up everywhere, even in her desire to buy a newer, fancier car. She really wanted it, but every time she thought about moving forward, that old voice came in. "You have enough. You don't need it." It was such a familiar story in her life: wanting more, but stopping herself just before allowing it in.

So every time Dianne went to raise her rates, launch something new, or let herself dream bigger, that same old programming whispered, "Be careful, don't be greedy, you already have enough."

It's not sabotage, it's protection. The subconscious isn't trying to hurt us. It's trying to keep us safe. But safe often looks like staying small.

Once Dianne saw that belief for what it was, we used tapping to help her release it. As she moved through the tapping protocol, her energy began to soften. We replaced those old thoughts with new truths:

"I can be rich and kind."

"I can have enough and still receive more."

"I can be successful without taking from anyone else."

By the end, she took a deep breath and said, "Wow, I feel like I can finally take my foot off the brake."

And that's what happens when you start flipping the thoughts that have been quietly running the show. You free yourself to move forward with ease, confidence, and flow.

And that kind of shift doesn't just happen inside my Accelerator. I've seen it unfold right in the middle of a live workshop, where the energy in the room begins to transform.

I remember the day vividly. I was invited to speak about Dishing the T-E-A in person to a room of women CEOs. By the end of the workshop, one woman, Rose, was in tears.

She told me, "I was feeling so bad I didn't even want to come today, but I'm so glad I did. Your training completely changed my energy."

In that moment, I felt myself choke up. I've been there, in that place of not wanting to show up, of feeling heavy and stuck. What struck me most was how quickly everything shifted for her. In less than an hour, she went from hopelessness to hope.

That's the power of what you're learning here. Rose reminded me why I do this work, because women already have the power inside them; they just need the tools to access it. Transformation doesn't have to take months or years. It can happen in minutes when you change the thought that starts the chain.

If we mapped Rose's experience onto TEAR, it would look like this: a heavy, defeating Thought ("I don't even want to go") created a low Emotion (hopelessness), which nearly led to the Action of not showing up and the predictable Result of staying stuck. But by entering the room and engaging with a new thought, her emotion lifted, her actions opened, and her result changed in real time. That's what flipping the "T" can do. If you want different results, you don't start with action. You start with the thought.

A client, Autumn, had been carrying around the thought "I'm not good enough" for years. It was so familiar, she didn't even notice it anymore, like an old handbag slung over her shoulder, filled with stale mints, crumpled receipts, and forgotten stories she no longer needed to hold.

Every time business slowed down or clients didn't respond right away, that handbag would slip back onto her arm. She would think, "Maybe I'm not that good" or "Maybe they don't want to work with me again." She knew logically it wasn't true.

She had great testimonials and many years of professional proof, but emotionally, it still felt heavy.

During one of our coaching calls, we used tapping to move the energy around that belief. As we went through the tapping protocol, she began to laugh, picturing the old handbag in vivid detail. "I don't even want to donate this one," she said. "I want to burn it." And that's exactly what we did. Energetically, she let it go.

Moments later, she remembered an email from a client thanking her for a life-changing workshop, and a message from another asking to rebook. It was as if the universe had been waiting for her to drop the old bag before handing her a new one, a beautiful, elegant purse filled with proof of her brilliance and worth.

She decided to make a ritual out of it. Every time she receives a thank-you note, a testimonial, or a text of appreciation, she prints it or writes it down and puts it in her "new bag." It's her reminder that the story of "not enough" no longer belongs to her.

If we mapped Autumn's shift onto the TEAR model, it would look like this:

Her original Thought, "I'm not good enough," created Emotions of doubt and insecurity, which led to Actions like discounting or hesitating to follow up, and the Result was inconsistency. After releasing the energy with tapping, we flipped the thought to "I create transformation, and I'm worthy of my rates." Her emotions lifted to confidence, her actions became bold and aligned, and her results followed suit.

And in this chapter, we're going to pull back the curtain on the thoughts you've been letting run your show. We're going to look at the beliefs that feel like truth but are really just fear in disguise. We're going to talk about how to catch them and replace them with something that actually gets you where you want to go.

Once you see how this works, you'll never look at your thoughts and your life the same way, thank goodness. Because, Abundant B, you were meant for more. I know it.

Most of the thoughts you think every single day aren't even yours. They're old programming. Stories you picked up from your parents, teachers, friends, or society before you even knew how to question them.

Science tells us we have about 80,000 thoughts a day. And the wild part is, 95% of them come from our subconscious mind. That's the part of our brain that was mostly formed before the age of seven. Which means, unless you've done the work to rewire it, there's a seven-year-old running your business and your bank account.

Let's think about that for a moment, Abundant B. Your seven-year-old self, whose biggest concerns were snack time and whether your best friend still liked you, is the one deciding if you raise your prices, say yes to the big opportunity, or take the scary leap. No wonder fear creeps in.

Actually, the subconscious isn't trying to hurt you; it's trying to protect you. Its job is to keep you safe and comfortable. And comfortable often means familiar, because the subconscious finds change very scary. Which is why we repeat the same habits, attract the same money patterns, and replay the same damn stories over and over again.

The problem is, often the familiar doesn't mean abundance for you.

Here is where it gets really interesting, Abundant B. You have something in your brain called the Reticular Activating System, or RAS. It's like your brain's personal filter, a VIP bouncer, deciding who, or what in this case, gets in and gets turned away at the door.

You can also think of RAS like the algorithm in your favorite social media app. Whatever you engage with most is what it keeps showing you. Click on a few videos of puppies? Suddenly, your feed is full of adorable dogs. The same thing happens with your thoughts. Focus on "clients are hard to find," and your RAS will serve you endless proof that it's true. Sucks, right? But focus on "money flows to me easily," and your RAS will start looking for ways to prove that right instead. Isn't that fun?!

Listen, this isn't just a cute metaphor; it's how your brain is running the show every single day. Your subconscious mind is a total overachiever. Scientists estimate it processes information up to 500,000 times faster than your conscious mind. It's constantly scanning, sorting, and filtering, taking in millions of bits of information every second, but letting in only a tiny fraction into your conscious awareness. That's why you can drive home without remembering half the trip, or find yourself humming a song you didn't even notice was playing in the background. Your brain is basically a high-speed supercomputer, and you're the one typing in the search terms through your thoughts.

And your brain loves patterns, familiarity, and efficiency. It will always look for proof of what it already believes. If you've been telling yourself for years that "money is hard to make," your brain will happily go, "Got it, boss!" and find endless evidence to support that belief, because it's easier than creating a new pattern. However, good news, the opposite is also true. Give your brain a new story to work with, and it will go to work finding proof of that instead.

Let's play this out. Let's say you believe, "No one is buying right now." Your RAS will notice every post, article, podcast, or friend where someone complains about how slow sales are.

You will also completely miss the Instagram story of the coach who just sold out her program. And maybe even scroll right past the email from someone asking to work with you because your brain didn't flag it as important. Flip that belief to "my work is in demand" or "everyone wants to work with me," and your RAS gets a whole new set of instructions. Suddenly, you notice a DM from someone asking about your services. You overhear a conversation at a coffee shop that sparks an idea for a collaboration. A past client reaches out "out of the blue" to rehire you.

It may seem like magic, and it kind of is, but it's also the mechanics of your brain. Your brain will always find what you've trained it to look for. So why not train it to look for evidence that you're magnetic, in-demand, and wildly talented?

So my challenge to you is to start noticing TODAY. Pay attention to where your thoughts automatically go and what patterns you see.

Are you scanning for problems or possibilities?

Proof you're failing, or proof you're thriving?

Reasons to pull back, or reasons to lean in?

Are you looking for roadblocks… or are you actively looking for opportunities to grow, connect, and receive?

The way you answer that tells you exactly what your subconscious and your RAS are serving up on repeat. And once you see it, you can change it. And when you do, buckle up Abundant B, because your reality won't just shift, it'll start dancing to a whole new beautiful beat.

Now that you're starting to notice your thoughts, let's talk about what happens next because those thoughts don't just float around in your head doing nothing. They trigger feelings, lots of them. And this is the E in TEAR: Emotions.

Every person has a different reaction to the exact same event. You and I could be in the same place at the same time, hearing and seeing the exact same thing, and yet we'd feel something completely different. Why? Because our emotional reaction isn't based on the event itself, it's based on our internal programming. The event is actually neutral.

Your brain takes what's happening around you, runs it through all your beliefs, past experiences, and stored memories, and then hands you an emotion. That's why two people can sit in the same meeting and have different feelings about it. One may be thinking, "This is so exciting, I can't wait to share my ideas," while the other is silently panicking, "They're going to realize I don't belong here." All in the same room, same conversation, but with completely different emotions.

Let me give you a business example. Imagine you launch a new offer, and it's been two days with zero sign-ups. One business owner might immediately think, "This was a bad idea. No one wants this. I should have priced it lower." Those thoughts trigger emotions like shame, anxiety, and defeat. Another business owner in the exact same situation might think, "People are still seeing it. Sales often happen at the last minute. I'm going to keep showing up. The race isn't over yet, it's only just beginning." Those thoughts trigger emotions like confidence, trust, and determination.

Same event, two days with no sales. Totally different emotional experience depending on their own thoughts, beliefs, and programming. And those emotions will drive two very different sets of reactions, causing different actions (or inactions). The first business owner might start discounting, stop talking about the offer, or disappear entirely. The second will keep showing up, keep sharing, and likely create the sales they want.

And the kicker, Abundant B? Emotions aren't random. They're the direct result of your thoughts. A thought like "clients are ghosting me" might trigger anxiety, frustration, or self-doubt. But a thought like "the right clients are always on their way to me" might trigger excitement, trust, or motivation.

That shift in emotion is everything because your emotions determine the energy you're broadcasting. And that energy? It's contagious. It's what people feel from you before you even say a word.

We'll go deeper into energy in the next chapter. But for now, we're still sipping on the "T" for Thoughts, because they are the foundation. Without mastering your thoughts, your energy and alignment don't stand a chance of creating the abundance you're calling in.

And here's where things start to move, Abundant B, because your emotions don't just sit there looking pretty. They drive what you do next. This is the A in TEAR: Actions.

When you're feeling confident, inspired, and hopeful, you show up differently. You send the pitch. You follow up with the client. You write the post with boldness. You walk into the room as if you belong there. You radiate energy that makes people want to be around you.

But when you're feeling anxious, defeated, or resentful? You avoid hard conversations. You procrastinate. You second-guess yourself. You play small. Your actions shrink to match the smallness of the emotion that created them.

Abundant B, you can be "doing all the things" on paper, but if the energy fueling those actions is desperation, doubt, or fear, people will feel it. On the flip side, even small actions taken from an empowered belief can create massive ripple effects.

Taking action from faith instead of fear leads to more fun!

And now we've hit the R in TEAR: the result. This is the part everyone obsesses over, but Abundant B, the results are not the starting point. They are the outcomes for the way you've been thinking, feeling, and acting. They're proof of what's been going on behind the scenes in your mind and your energy.

The money in your account right now? The clients in your calendar? The opportunities flowing your way (or not)? These results are all a reflection of the chain reaction you've been running in your subconscious and your conscious mind. The thoughts → emotions → actions. If you don't like a result, you don't beat yourself up. You don't need to start frantically doing more. All you need to do is go back to the beginning and change the thought (or thoughts) that have been running the show.

And let me tell you, Abundant B, when you upgrade your thoughts, your emotions rise to match. When your emotions rise, your actions get bolder, braver, more magnetic. And when that happens? Your results shift dramatically, sometimes so fast it'll make your head spin.

Your results are simply the mirror. Change what's inside, and the reflection will change.

Sounds simple, right? Change the thought. Well, it sounds easier than it is. Don't worry, Abundant B, I'm here to guide you through this. Because once you learn how to spot those sneaky, unhelpful thoughts and swap them for beliefs that actually serve you, you'll unlock a level of power you didn't even know you had.

Here's how the TEAR model is simplified in real life:

- **Thoughts.** These are the starting points. Every single result you have right now began with a thought, whether you realized it or not. Sometimes they're loud and obvious, and sometimes they're those quiet, background beliefs you've been carrying since childhood.

- **Emotions.** Your thoughts send a signal to your body that creates a feeling. Think *"I'm behind"* and you'll probably feel anxious or rushed. Think *"I'm right on track"* and you'll likely feel calm and confident.

- **Actions.** Your emotions are what get you moving (or keep you frozen). When you feel inspired, excited, or determined, you're more likely to take bold, aligned action. When you feel scared or doubtful, you might procrastinate, avoid, or make fear-based decisions.

- **Results.** These are simply the byproducts of the first three steps. Your bank balance, your client list, and your business growth are all feedback from the thoughts, emotions, and actions you've been running on repeat.

So, if you want to change your results, you don't have to work harder, hustle more, or "figure it all out" overnight. You simply start at the top and ask: What thought is creating this chain reaction?

From there, you can start shifting the thought, which shifts the emotion, which shifts the action, which, you guessed it, changes the result.

And if you ever feel stuck, like you can't quite get to a new thought, that's where EFT tapping comes in. Tapping is one of my favorite tools for shifting the energy around a thought you've been looping in your head. It stops you in your tracks. It helps release the resistance in your body so you can actually come up with and believe a new thought you're choosing. We'll go deeper into this in Chapter 8.

And here's the magic, Abundant B: The more you practice this, the faster the shifts happen. At first, it might take a few days to catch the thought and change it. Eventually, you'll be flipping your thoughts and your results in minutes like a well-oiled machine.

THE ABUNDANT B FLIP-THE-SCRIPT EXERCISE

For the next 48 hours, I want you to play detective with your thoughts. Keep a small notebook or note on your phone and write down any thought that feels heavy, limiting, or just plain unhelpful. Don't judge it, just capture it.

Once you have a few, go back and ask yourself: What's a more empowering, Abundant B version of this thought? Write those down too.

Example:

Limiting thought: "No one is going to buy my offer."

Abundant B thought: "The right people are finding me every day, and they can't wait to work with me."

Limiting thought: "I never have enough time."

Abundant B thought: "I always have time for what matters most, and everything gets done in perfect timing."

Do this for at least three thoughts a day for the next two days. The more you practice, the easier it will be to catch yourself in the moment and flip the thought right then and there. I also want you to see how powerful this can be when it's put into action, so let me share a few examples from clients who've done exactly this.

One client, named Ashley, had proven she could create big income months of $20K, sometimes more, but every time it happened, she ended up exhausted and flirting with burnout. Deep down, she believed the only way to sustain that level of income was to sacrifice her health and mental well-being. Her thought was, "I can't make this money every month without running myself into the ground." That belief created fear and hesitation, which led her to pull back on offers and unintentionally stall her own growth. When we began shifting her thoughts to, "It's possible I can make this money with ease. Maybe it could even be easier than last time," everything changed. Her fear softened into curiosity and hope. She began acting from faith instead of fear, and better yet, started having fun! She also started restructuring her offers and protecting her time, and the money flowed in without the exhaustion.

Another client, Julie, was convinced she didn't have the discipline or stamina to maintain a six-figure business. Her thought was, "I'm slower than everyone else, and I can't keep up." That belief created frustration and shame, which kept her stuck in a cycle of starting projects but never finishing them, constantly comparing herself to others, and avoiding bigger goals. When she began telling herself, "I can do this without it being draining. This could feel easier than I think," her emotions shifted to possibility, and she started showing up consistently, finishing what she started, and taking bold action. The results followed quickly, and her business revenue began climbing toward six figures.

And then there was the client who almost talked herself out of working with her dream client. When the opportunity came, Darlene's thoughts spiraled. "They won't pay my rates. I might mess it up. I'm afraid I'll let them down." Her emotions were pure anxiety, and her actions reflected that anxiety: she avoided responding, downplayed her value, and sidestepped a direct conversation about money. We shifted the thought (with a little help from some EFT tapping) to, "I am good enough. I have the skills and experience to deliver." Her fear turned into grounded confidence. She reached out, presented her offer at full price, and her client said yes happily.

These are the kinds of shifts that happen when you start catching the thought, flipping it, and letting that new belief create a different chain reaction.

And here's what I want you to remember, Abundant B: you can do this too. You are already capable of catching the thoughts that have been running the show and choosing new ones that align with the woman you're becoming. You don't have to get it perfect. You don't have to do it all at once. Every single time you catch a thought and flip it, you're rewiring your brain step by step, raising your energy, and shifting the path of your entire future. This is how change starts. This is how you step into your next level of abundance.

You already have everything it takes to think like the abundant, magnetic, wealthy woman you truly are, and now you have the tools to start doing it on purpose. We've just covered the "T" in Dishing the TEA, your Thoughts, which also happens to be the T in the TEAR model and the first step to attracting more abundance into your life and business.

Your thoughts are the starting line for everything you'll ever attract.

When you learn to flip them on purpose, you change the entire trajectory of what flows to you.

Now it's time to pour in the next ingredient, the "E," which is all about your Energy. In the next chapter, we'll explore how your energy impacts your abundance, unpack the Emotional Scale, and show you exactly how to raise your vibration so the results you desire have no choice but to find you. When your energy rises, your results rise too, and that's when the magic starts pouring in.

chapter four

THE "E" IN TEA:
THE ENERGY OF ABUNDANCE

In the last chapter, we explored how your thoughts shape your beliefs, your behaviors, and ultimately your abundance, but that is only part of the equation. Now it's time to stir in the "E" in Dishing the T-E-A. The E is for your Energy.

Energy is the frequency you're operating from, the emotional state you live in most of the time. It's either aligned with abundance or resisting it. And as an Abundant B, your energy is everything. You don't manifest by pushing harder. You manifest by harmonizing with abundance and joy, by choosing to feel good and shifting your inner state, no matter what's happening outside of you. And I know this because I've lived it.

When I made the decision I talked about in Chapter 1 to let go of my last CFO client, I was terrified. I knew in my gut it was the right move, but that didn't mean the fear disappeared. I had released the safety net of consistent income, and even though I had savings, the part of me wired for survival was screaming, "What if this doesn't work?"

Here is the truth. I didn't hustle my way through it. I knew manifesting was all about shifting my energy, so that is what I did.

I immersed myself in the Emotional Scale, first introduced by Abraham Hicks. You can get your free copy of the Emotional Scale inside the book portal if you'd like one to print out.

You'll find a copy for your reference on the following page.

I knew that if I could stay in the top half 51% of the time, I could stay in alignment with what I wanted to create. Even if fear was still present, I could choose to feel gratitude and appreciation that I had the financial security to make this leap. I could also feel excitement about what was coming. I could tune into hope and belief, even if I couldn't yet see the how.

And so I did. I made it my full-time job to shift my emotional state.

I would recognize the fear when it crept in and choose a better thought. I would journal about my dreams of this new business and vision. I would start tapping anytime fear would creep in and shift my emotional energy. You'll learn more about tapping (Emotional Freedom Technique) in Chapter 8.

I said to myself, *How does it feel to already have the life and business I dreamed of?* And not through force or overworking, which was what my old self would have done. I wanted to create a life of alignment and fun. A business I was excited to go to work at every day. What did that look and feel like?

EMOTIONAL SCALE*

JOY / APPRECIATION / EMPOWERED / FREEDOM / LOVE

PASSION

ENTHUSIASM / EAGERNESS / HAPPINESS

POSITIVE EXPECTATION / BELIEF

OPTIMISM

HOPEFULNESS

SATISFACTION / CONTENTMENT

▲ GOAL: TRY TO STAY IN THIS ENERGY 51% OF THE TIME TO MAXIMIZE MANIFESTATION

BOREDOM

PESSIMISM

FRUSTRATION / IRRITATION / IMPATIENCE

OVERWHELMED

DISAPPOINTMENT

DOUBT

WORRY

BLAME

DISCOURAGEMENT

ANGER

REVENGE

HATRED / RAGE

JEALOUSY

INSECURITY / GUILT / UNWORTHINESS

FEAR / GRIEF / DEPRESSION / DESPAIR / POWERLESSNESS

*Inspired by the Emotional Guidance Scale by Esther and Jerry Hicks (Abraham-Hicks Publications), whose work has deeply influenced my own teachings.

Every day, I showed up for the inner work of staying in high-vibe energy and reprogramming my beliefs. Let me be clear, I required a shit ton of belief reprogramming. And then, two and a half weeks in, it happened.

I manifested $29,000.

Random checks arrived in the mail. One for $8,000, one for $16,000, and a $5,000 deposit showed up in my personal bank account. None of it was expected, and none of it was from my business, which actually made it better because it reminded me to let go of the "how." The universe was showing me: Yes, this works. Keep going.

I felt this assurance not just in my mind, but in my body and in my soul. I knew I was on to something. I was happy. I was energized and totally freaking lit up. And it was the most money I had ever manifested out of thin air. It blew my mind.

Really, though, it wasn't out of thin air. It was emotional alignment. It was gratitude, excitement, and a decision to trust and surrender to the belief that something better, more fun, more abundant was on its way. And it was. I finally understood what it all meant. It only took me 50+ years.

Most people spend their time below the energy line, but awareness is everything. Take a moment to review the energy scale. How often are you staying above the energy line? I could have stayed in the fear energy. But I choose differently, because fear is the lowest form of energy on the Emotional Scale. And if I had stayed in that energy, it would have sent me spiraling and kept me from manifesting the money that I did.

I'm not going to tell you it was easy to shift out of fear. This isn't about perfection; it's about practice. I still wobble. I still have moments of doubt and fear. The difference is, I know how to change. I come back to this because it works. And that is what matters.

Here are a few quick ways to shift your energy and start climbing the Emotional Scale, one intentional step at a time. And the first step? Energetic awareness.

Not what you're thinking, but what you're feeling.

Most of us don't even realize when we've dropped into fear, frustration, or doubt. We're so used to pushing through that we forget to check in with the vibe we're carrying. But as an Abundant B, your energy is your magnet. It's what sets the tone for everything you attract. That's why energy work begins with simply noticing where your energy is.

Notice how you feel in your body. Notice what kind of energy you're bringing into your day, your decisions, your money, and your business. Most of us live on emotional autopilot. We're so used to powering through and pushing harder that we don't even stop to feel what we're actually feeling. But your energy doesn't lie, and it doesn't wait for a to-do list. It responds to how you feel at any given moment.

So check in with yourself. How do you feel at this moment? Where does that emotion land on the Emotional Scale? Is it helping you attract more of what you want, or is it keeping you stuck in the same low-energy cycle?

There's no judgment here, only awareness. Because the moment you become aware, you gain the power to shift.

And the cool thing is: once you start shifting your energy, not only will you attract more abundance, but people will also begin to notice. I had people I hadn't seen in months, even years, tell me they could see something different. "You're glowing," they'd say. "Your energy feels so good." And it wasn't just people I knew. Strangers started saying it too. "I don't know what it is, but I love your energy." That had never happened to me before. Not once. And now? I hear it all the time. And guess what? I love my energy too.

Now that you're aware of where your energy is on the Emotional Scale, it's time for the next step, energy shifting. There are so many ways to shift your energy. For me, if I feel myself lowering on the Emotional Scale, it's often as simple as walking in nature, sitting in the sun for five minutes, or blasting a song that lights me up. Sometimes it's dancing. Sometimes it's deep breathing or meditating. Sometimes it's laughing with and having fun with my grandkids. It doesn't have to be complicated; it just has to be intentional.

Another thing I like to do is bring in gratitude. Yes, gratitude is one of the fastest ways to raise your vibration. Even just a few moments of appreciation can help you move up the scale. In Part Four, I'll give you a list of 70 simple energy-shifting prompts that you can use anytime you feel yourself spiraling. I use these as daily prompts with my clients in the Money Mindset and Manifestation Accelerator.

Right now, I simply want you to notice what lifts you. What lights you up? What makes you feel even slightly more open, grounded, or energized?

Because your energy is always available to recalibrate. No matter what's happening around you. No matter how heavy things feel. You're not here to live stuck at the bottom of the scale. You're an Abundant B. You're here to feel good and to harmonize with the life you're calling in.

One thing I've learned over and over again is this: Your energy isn't just some spiritual concept. It's real, and it affects everything: how you feel, how you show up, and what flows in (or doesn't).

I used to lead with strategy first. If a mentor told me to use a specific marketing or sales strategy to attract clients, whether it felt aligned or not, I followed their suggestions. That was my comfort zone, pushing through my discomfort instead of asking myself, "Does this align with who I am?" And honestly? That part of me still exists. I still love strategy, but now I start with energy—every time.

I know when my energy is off. When I'm tired, misaligned, or pushing too hard, it doesn't matter how good the strategy is. When things feel stuck or forced, or like I'm doing everything "right" and still not seeing results, I check in, or check out, and take a break.

I'll ask myself, is this strategy aligned with who I am? Or is this someone else's strategy I'm trying to force to make it work? What would feel good right now? What's the most aligned next step, not the most logical?

This is what I mean when I say energy first, strategy second. It has to be aligned with you, how you want to show up, and who you want to be.

Don't get me wrong, it's not about throwing the structure out. It's about letting your energy lead. That's when things click into place.

It's also important to know that raising your energy frequency isn't always about adding more. It's also about noticing what's draining you and changing it.

Sometimes the fastest shift is removing what's pulling you down, things you've been tolerating, commitments that no longer fit, people who don't respect you or your boundaries, or even habits that keep you stuck in a lower energetic state. It could be comparison, second-guessing, or overthinking. It could be trying to please everyone at the expense of yourself (I see you, Abundant B).

Pay attention to what feels heavy. Maybe it's frustration, or perhaps it's numbness. You'll feel it in your body. Not the tightness that comes from fear, that can be expansive. I'm talking about heaviness and flatness. The tightness of fear can be good, and you can get to the other side of that. It is the flatness that's your sign that something's out of alignment.

Energy is subtle, but it's also incredibly loud when you start listening to it.

You don't have to be perfect with this. I'm not. I still catch myself spiraling. I still have days (even weeks) where my energy dips and everything feels hard. But now I know how to recognize it quicker. And I know how to come back from it. And that's what makes the difference.

You're not meant to live at the bottom of the Emotional Scale. You're meant to feel good. You're meant to feel supported. And you get to build your business and your life from that place, not from dread, pressure, or burnout.

This is what it means to be in your Abundant B energy.

This played out for me in real-time recently. I had just wrapped a launch for my Money Mindset and Manifestation Accelerator, a three-month live group experience where we do EFT tapping, focus on our energy, and improve our money mindset. I was proud of it. I showed up fully. I believed in the offer and the women it was for. But when the doors closed, the numbers weren't what I had hoped for. And I'll be honest, I felt a little off. Like something just wasn't clicking the way it normally does. So I listened to my energy and gave myself a break.

I booked a last-minute trip to my favorite place, Naples, Florida. I usually don't head down there until November for the winter, but it was early September, and I just felt the pull to go. I needed space, some white sand, and sunshine. I wanted to get my feet in the water, breathe in the salty air, and reset.

What I didn't realize was that just by saying yes to what felt good, my energy had already shifted. On the very first day, literally, with my toes in the sand, two things happened. One of my private coaching clients reached out and said she was ready to move forward and work together. Minutes later, I got a text about a speaking opportunity.

And by the end of that week, while I was "off" from business, not only one, but two new clients and two new speaking opportunities came in, just like that: no forcing, no pushing, pure alignment, pure miracle.

I didn't pitch for any of them. I didn't follow up or push. I was just in my happy place. And the opportunities showed up. That's the difference energy makes.

It wasn't a strategy or hustle; it was 100% energy shift and pure ease. And it came after I let go of the pressure and came back to what lights me up. That's the power of your energy and how it can completely change your results. Energy shifts everything: your results, your relationships, your business, your income—all of it.

Let me give you another example of how this works, one I know you'll relate to.

Think back to high school or your early twenties. Remember when you were dating someone, and they broke up with you? You were heartbroken. Devastated. Maybe even a little obsessed. Perhaps even tried to win them back, but nothing worked.

Fast forward a few months or a year or more. You meet someone new. You move on. You start falling in love again, the kind of love that lights you up and makes you feel good all over. You stop thinking about the ex entirely.

And then what happens? Boom. Out of nowhere, they reappear—the ex. The one who ghosted you or left you hanging suddenly wants you back. You didn't text them. You didn't reach out. You didn't do anything. But you shifted your energy. You were happy, confident, and in love. Radiating a whole new frequency.

And that frequency? It did its job. It attracted, it manifested, and pulled things to you.

I remember this happening to me more than once. And I remember thinking, What the hell? Why now? I was finally feeling good, and now I have to make a decision?

That's what your energy does. It speaks for you. You don't have to chase; you get to attract. You don't have to prove or force; you get to trust, magnetize, and receive.

You just have to shift into the frequency of what you actually want and let the universe do its magic.

Let this be your reminder that positive energy is available to you in every moment. You don't need hours of meditation or a perfectly curated routine to shift it. You just need a little awareness and a willingness to come back to yourself.

Sometimes it's a breath of fresh air and a little sunshine. It could be your favorite music. Or maybe it's walking away from your laptop and putting your bare feet on the earth. Whatever brings you back to your power, that's your portal.

For me, it's movement, music, nature, and laughter. A deep belly laugh will raise your vibration faster than any strategy spreadsheet. It's the realignment back to joy, which is the truest frequency of abundance.

And remember, you don't need to leap from fear to joy in one big jump. You just need to reach for something a little lighter. A little more hopeful. That's how you climb the Emotional Scale one gentle step at a time.

We'll go deeper into how to shift your energy in the next chapter, because energy without alignment is like turning on a magnet and pointing it in the wrong direction. But for now, just remember this:

Your energy sets the tone. It's the signal you send out into the world before you say a word or take a single action. You don't need to hustle harder; all you need to do is elevate your energy. You are the whole damn signal. And the universe? She's listening.

Because you, my love, are an Abundant B.

Abundant B Prompt

Pause and journal on this:

What does it feel like when my energy is magnetic?

How do I know I'm aligned?

How does the version of me who attracts with ease show up in her day, her business, her life?

Abundant B Visualization

Close your eyes. Take a deep breath in through your nose, and let it out slowly through your mouth. Do that again, relax, be right here in the moment.

You've been doing a lot. But for the next minute, you don't have to do anything. You just get to be. Feel your body sink a little deeper into your seat. Let your shoulders drop. Let your jaw unclench. Let your breath become your anchor.

Now imagine you're standing in your highest energy—the version of you who feels lit up.

The one who trusts her desires. The one who knows she's magnetic. See her. Feel her. What is she wearing? Where is she standing? How does her body feel? Light, expansive? Alive and excited? Let that energy move through you now from the crown of your head, through your chest, down your spine, and into the earth beneath your feet. You don't have to earn this feeling.

You get to allow it. This is your natural Abundant B state, energized and in flow.

When you're ready, take one more breath and open your eyes. You just shifted your energy.

And that changes everything.

For an audio version of this visualization and much more, scan the QR CODE below to get free access to the book portal.

Abundant B Mantra

> My energy is magnetic. I trust, align, and receive with ease.

Know you're no longer the woman who waits for things to change before she feels good. You're the woman who shifts first. You hold the frequency of the woman you're becoming. A woman who knows who she is and knows her worth. And the world will respond.

Now that you've shifted your energy, it's time to make it real. To take action from a place that actually feels good to you. When your energy is dialed in and your actions are aligned, that's when it all clicks.

So let's keep going. In the next chapter, we'll unlock what alignment really means, not just as a concept, but as a way of doing business, making decisions, and showing up as the woman you're here to be. You've activated the energy. Now let's give it somewhere to flow.

chapter five

THE "A" IN TEA: ALIGNMENT CREATES MIRACLES

In the last chapter, we talked about your energy and how it attracts and magnetizes your results. But energy alone isn't enough. Now it's time to infuse the "A" in Dishing the T-E-A. The A is for Alignment. Your joy is not a bonus, it's a strategy. Alignment is where everything begins to click, where your desires, your actions, and your energy finally move in the same direction.

Alignment is where your inner truth meets your outer expression. It's the moment you stop hiding and begin to lead from wholeness and start bringing all of you to the work you do. The parts you are hiding will attract exactly who you are meant to serve. Trust that.

For a long time, I thought alignment meant doing what I was good at. I was great with numbers, I had built a very profitable multi-six-figure CFO practice, and I was helping businesses grow. On paper, it looked like success. But something was missing. I was checking all the boxes, but I wasn't lit up inside. Mondays didn't excite me. The work didn't make me feel expansive, it just felt like work.

Alignment comes from doing what you love, not just what you're good at, but what truly fills you up. It's the thing that makes you want to jump out of bed in the morning, excited to start your day. It's what has you saying, "I can't wait for Monday," instead of dreading the week ahead. It's the work that feels so natural and fulfilling that you'd do it for free (not that I want you to, but you would if I let you!). A true Abundant B is lit up from the inside out!

For me, alignment finally clicked when I stopped trying to hide the parts of myself I thought were "too much" or "too weird." For years, I kept my spiritual side separate from my business, terrified my CFO clients would judge me if they saw me pulling oracle cards, tapping through limiting beliefs, or talking about manifestation. So, I stayed in the logical, numbers-only lane. I wore a professional mask and left the magic in the closet.

But that was exhausting. I wasn't showing up as my whole self, and it kept me stuck in this cycle of feeling like something was always off. Everything changed the moment I decided to step fully into my identity as The Manifesting CFO. I gave myself permission to bring it all in: the strategy and the soul, the spreadsheets and the spirituality, the financial clarity and the fun. I wasn't just a logical CFO anymore. I was the woman who could help you shift your energy, coach you through money mindset blocks and limiting beliefs, pull a card for guidance, and still walk you through your Profit and Loss statement with confidence. And when I started bringing tapping into the money mindset, and abundance struggles my clients were facing, miracles happened. Beliefs that had held them back for years shifted in an instant, and the ripple effects showed up not just in their businesses, but in their lives.

What shocked me the most was how invigorated I felt. I was so excited to go to work every day. I couldn't wait to see who I was going to help shift beliefs in our group sessions. Sometimes they cried as the energy trapped in their bodies was finally released. And I was just as excited to watch what came after: the growth, the expansion, the prosperity in ways they hadn't thought possible before. It was pure magic, and I was exhilarated. That's what alignment feels like. It's a full YES in your body, and it feeds your energy and joy.

Stepping into this wholeness is exactly how the Money Mindset & Manifestation Accelerator was born. It came straight from alignment, no official launch, no sales page, just pure excitement and a clear yes in my body. I wanted 10 women. I was hoping for 15, but 20 stepped in. It was the easiest thing I had ever sold because it was the most authentic expression of my work.

Abundant B Prompt

Where am I hiding parts of myself in my brand or business?

When we talk about alignment, it's essential to notice the two core energies we all carry: the masculine and the feminine. And let me be clear, this has nothing to do with gender. These are simply two different ways that energy flows through us.

Masculine energy is focused, structured, and directional. It's the part of you that thrives on a plan, checks things off a list, and gets that satisfying rush from taking bold action. It's the voice inside that says, "Let's make this happen."

Feminine energy is intuitive, fluid, and creative. It's the part of you that can drop into a vision, trust your inner knowing, and receive support without guilt. It's the voice inside that says, "Let's feel into what's right." This is the flow.

Neither is better, and you need both. Think of the masculine as the riverbank and the feminine as the water. Without the banks, the water would spill everywhere. Without the water, the banks would sit dry and empty. Together, they create flow, movement, and direction.

For most of my life, I lived almost entirely in my masculine energy. I was the goal-driven high achiever who pushed through every ounce of discomfort just to get it done. And yes, it brought me a lot of success. But it only made me happy for a hot minute. The high would fade, burnout would creep in, and when things didn't move fast enough, I'd get frustrated, pissed, and push even harder. That was my pattern. And deep down, I knew there had to be an easier way.

When I finally gave myself permission to lean into my feminine, everything shifted. I started trusting my intuition instead of forcing every step. I allowed support in, instead of clinging to the belief that I had to do it all myself. I made space for joy, creativity, and rest. And guess what, the results actually came faster. The feminine softened the edges of my hustle and brought me back to ease. And most importantly, it kept me in the game.

But Abundant B, if you swing too far into feminine energy, you'll get stuck there too. Journaling, visualizing, and waiting for the universe to drop it in your lap won't create anything on its own. You can have the juiciest, most magnetic vision board in the world, but if you never send the email, launch the program, or make the hire, it stays just that, a vision. Too much flow without structure is like water with no banks. It feels good for a moment, but it runs all over the place and actually goes nowhere.

That's why balance is everything. The masculine builds the container, the feminine fills it with flow. The masculine gives you the structure, the feminine breathes life, color, and creativity into it. Alone, one will burn you out, and the other will leave you spinning your wheels. But together is where the magic happens. That's where you create aligned movement, momentum, and results that actually feel good, Abundant B.

Power is holding both the plan and the pleasure, the structure and the sparkle.

Abundant B Prompt

> Which energy do I default to most, masculine or feminine? How can I balance them?

Alignment isn't just something you think about; it's something you feel. You can't logic your way into alignment. You sense it. You know it in your body. That's where intuition comes in.

It's all part of your energy, and your body will tell you the truth long before your mind catches up. Remember some of the low-vibration feelings from the Emotional Scale? If you feel frustrated, bored, doubtful, disappointed, discouraged, or angry, you'll feel it in your body. Tight shoulders. Knots in your stomach. A heaviness in your chest. That could be a signal you're probably not aligned with what you're doing. Take the time and space to notice this.

On the other hand, when you're aligned, your body opens. You feel light, expansive, like you can breathe easier. Things feel exciting instead of heavy. You might even get those little tingles of energy, your intuition's way of saying, "Yes, this is it." And action doesn't feel like a grind anymore. It feels easy and fun. Like something you can't wait to do instead of something you have to do.

Alignment is clear. If it's not a "Hell Yes" in your body, then it's a no.

However, don't mistake alignment for the absence of fear. Fear can show up in your body too as shaky hands, butterflies, anxiety, or a racing heart. The difference is that alignment feels like a full body yes underneath the nerves, while misalignment feels like a hard no.

Abundant B Prompt

When I am making a decision, where in my body do I feel a full YES, and where do I feel a hard NO?

Learning to listen to your body is one way to recognize alignment. But the universe also loves to play with us, dropping little winks and nudges along the way. If you are paying attention, you will notice them. Feathers on the ground. Repeating numbers. Animals showing up in unexpected places. Even a random street sign with the exact word you needed to see. These signs are the universe's way of saying, "Yes, keep going" or "No, not that way."

I remember the first time a hawk came into my life. My mom was very ill, dying of cancer. I had stopped by her home to check on her, and that day her health was particularly bad. I wasn't sure she would see tomorrow. I was scared and sitting there alone with her. Then I looked out the window and saw a hawk perched on a telephone wire, staring directly at me. It felt like he was saying, "I've got you. You're strong. I'm here to get you through this." That hawk stayed for hours until my mom woke up again. From that day on, hawks became my sign. They now show up for me during big decisions and hard seasons, reminding me I am supported and never alone.

And it's not just me. My clients receive signs, too. My client, Lily, has the funniest story that shows just how playful the universe can be. She was contemplating a big move from London to York for her family, and she asked the universe to show her a dragonfly, her chosen sign, if it was the right decision. Now, dragonflies aren't exactly common in the middle of London, but one appeared right over her husband's head. Still, she wasn't convinced. So, she asked again, this time for a sign she absolutely could not miss. Soon after, while riding on the top of a double-decker bus with her mom, she looked up, and there it was, a literal street sign that said "York." You can't make this shit up. The universe was practically shouting at her, "Yes, this is your path."

And my client, Hailey, once chose a red cardinal as her sign. She wasn't seeing one outside, so she started to doubt whether her request would be answered. Later that day, she turned on the TV, and one of the people on the show was literally talking about red cardinals. That was her sign. The universe will always find a way to deliver, even through a conversation on a television show, if that's what it takes to get your attention.

I personally resonate most with animals, and I believe the universe knows that. If I see an unusual animal or a bunch of the same one at once, I take it as a message. I'll literally Google "spiritual meaning of seeing [insert animal]" to hear what guidance is coming through. Animals don't have to be your official sign to carry meaning. They can still show up as messengers. And remember, it doesn't have to be animals at all. There are so many ways to ask for and receive signs. The key is choosing what genuinely resonates with you.

So how do you ask for a sign? Simple. First, choose something meaningful. It could be an animal, a symbol, a word, or a number that feels special. Don't overthink it. Go with the first nudge. Then ask clearly: "If this is the right decision, show me a butterfly," or "If I'm on the right path, let me see 444." Then release it. Don't obsess over looking for it. Signs of love tend to show up when you least expect them.

Now the fun part. The universe has a sense of humor. Your sign might pop up on a billboard, in a song lyric, on the side of a bus, or on your friend's shirt. Stay open and trust what you receive. If you see your sign and feel that little spark in your body, that's alignment. That's your confirmation. You'll know it's for you when you see it.

Alignment isn't only what you feel inside. It's also how the world mirrors your energy back to you. The signs you receive remind you that when you're tuned in, the universe is tuned in with you. Alignment opens the door for guidance to flow in ways that are both mystical and very practical.

For me, one way I stay aligned is by walking in nature every morning. For 60 to 90 minutes, I give myself space to breathe, clear my mind, and shift my energy before the day begins. I almost always receive a sign. One morning, there was a plethora of ladybugs, which symbolize good luck. Another day, a parade of bunnies, one by one, crossed my path. I often see yellow finches fluttering around me, a sign of prosperity. These aren't just beautiful moments. They are reminders that I'm supported, I'm tuned in, and my energy is aligned before I ever sit down at my desk.

Alignment isn't perfection by any means. It's returning to a home feeling inside yourself. Giving yourself daily chances to tune back in. The more you practice, the more natural it becomes. You'll notice misalignment faster and bring yourself back with ease.

Let's dream for a moment. Imagine your business fully aligned with who you are. What would it look like? What work would you do? Who would you serve? How would your days feel if everything was a full body YES? This is the vision you're moving toward, little by little, every time you choose alignment over forcing, faith over fear, and flow over hustle.

Abundant B Prompt

> If my business were 100% aligned with who I am, what would it look and feel like? What would I need to change for full alignment?

So many entrepreneurs get stuck here. They buy the course, join the mastermind, hire the coach, and then try to copy and paste someone else's system exactly as it was taught. And when it doesn't work for them? They assume they're the problem. They think they must not be good enough, smart enough, or disciplined enough. And that's when many women quit the game altogether. It's not because they aren't capable, but because they were trying to play by someone else's rules.

But Abundant B's don't look at failure the way the world does. In fact, we don't even call it failure. It's all an experiment. Some things work, some things don't. Either way, you learn. Sure, you might get frustrated, maybe even cry a little. But then you pick yourself up, dust yourself off, and try again.

That's the most challenging part of entrepreneurship. Everyone thinks success happens overnight for some people, but what you don't see are all the late-night ugly cries, the moments of searching job ads, thinking maybe you should just quit and go back to the soul-sucking 9–5 gig. No one said this path would be easy. It's far from easy. And this is why alignment is so damn important. Because if you don't love what you're building, it will suck the life out of you until you give up.

The only way to fail is to give up.

THE ABUNDANT B REWRITE STRATEGY EXERCISE

Think of something a coach, mentor, or friend once told you to do in your business that didn't help. Maybe it's working great for them, but for you? It just feels heavy. Frustrating. Like, no matter how hard you try, your energy is off.

For me, it was the open-cart/close-cart launch model. Every coach swore by it. "You need scarcity. You have to give people a deadline, or they won't buy." So, I tried it. And honestly? It felt like total bullshit energy. Sending relentless emails, hyping up the "doors are closing" moment, only to feel the big letdown when I didn't hit the numbers I hoped for. And the truth was, everyone knew I'd open the program again later. It felt like a lie. My energy hated it, and that was the energy I was putting out into the world.

What I actually wanted was steady enrollment and aligned sales without all the drama. So, I rewrote it. Instead of pretending there was only one chance to join, I opened the doors and let women step in when they were ready. That shift felt light, honest, and expansive. And the wild part? It worked better. My results improved because I was finally selling in a way that aligned with me and my energy.

Now, grab your journal and ask yourself:

When I think about a strategy that doesn't feel like me, what result am I actually trying to create with this?

What are three other ways I could get the same result in a way that feels fun, exciting, or more aligned for me?

This is alignment in action. You're not throwing out the strategy, you're rewriting the rules so they work for YOU.

Abundant B Mantra

The only strategy that works is the one I love showing up for.

THE ABUNDANT B HELL YES DECISION EXERCISE

When you're faced with a decision, whether it's launching a program, saying yes to a new client, hiring a coach, or even choosing how to spend your afternoon, run it through this quick Hell Yes test.

Does it light me up?

Does it move me closer to my goals and who I want to be?

Does it feel like flow rather than force?

If you can say "Hell Yes" to all three, it passes. If not, it's not aligned.

Abundant B Mantra

If it's not a Hell Yes, it's a NO.

ABUNDANT B ALIGNMENT VISUALIZATION

Close your eyes and take a deep breath in, hold it, release. One more time, deep breath in, hold, release. Now feel yourself relax more and more with every breath you take. Let your shoulders drop, and your jaw soften.

Imagine waking up tomorrow to a life and business fully aligned with who you are. You stretch, smile, and feel excited for the day ahead. There's no dread, no forcing, only anticipation and joy of what the day holds.

See yourself walking into your workspace. Notice what's around you. The colors. The light. The energy. Everything in this space feels like you. You are so happy and excited to be there.

Now open your calendar for the day. You can't believe your eyes. Every appointment, every task, every client energizes. You feel expansive and grateful that this is how you get to spend your time.

Notice how your body feels in this aligned reality. Maybe there's a spring in your step, a smile you can't wipe off your face, or a calm wave of ease flowing through you. That's your whole body, YES.

Now ask yourself. What is one shift I can make today to bring myself closer to this aligned version of me and my business? Trust the first answer that comes. Feel into this excitement.

Take one more deep breath and let it anchor in. When you're ready, open your eyes and write down what came through.

For the audio version of the visualization above, please visit my book portal:

Alignment isn't about instant perfection. It's about practice. There will be days you feel unstoppable, and there will be days when things feel heavy or off. That doesn't mean you're failing; it means you're human. The real Abundant B power is noticing when you've drifted out of alignment and choosing to come back, again and again.

As I mentioned before, for me, spending time in my happy place on Naples beach always brings me back into alignment. When I give myself that space, miracles start happening. In fact, I wrote this very chapter at the beach in complete, Abundant B energy.

You now have tools to guide you. The Abundant B Rewrite for strategy, The Abundant B Hell Yes Test for decisions, and your own body and intuition as a compass. Layer in the signs, the daily practices, and the visualizations, and you'll start to notice how quickly you can shift back into flow.

Remember: alignment is what keeps you in the game when things get hard. It's what turns tears into breakthroughs, "failures" into lessons, and strategy into something that actually feels fun.

Every time you choose alignment over forcing, faith over fear, and flow over hustle, you're building a business and a life that excites you. And that's the essence of being an Abundant B — fully yourself, fully alive, and fully aligned.

Abundant B, you've just sipped the full cup of TEA — your Thoughts, your Energy, and your Alignment. These aren't just concepts; they're the foundation of everything you create. When even one of them is off, life feels flat, heavy, or forced. But when they're all working together? Miracles roll in. That's when money flows, opportunities chase you, and the abundance never stops!

And this is just the beginning. Because now, we're moving into the fun part: Creating abundance on autopilot. In the next section, I'm going to show you how to take everything you've learned so far and turn it into money, wealth, and overflow you can see in your bank account. (Ka-ching!) It's about to get really juicy.

part Three

CREATING ABUNDANCE:
WHERE FINANCIAL STRATEGY
MEETS SPIRITUAL POWER

chapter six

NUMBERS DON'T BITE—CLARITY CREATES CASH (KA-CHING)

Stop hiding from your numbers because clarity isn't scary, it's cash in the bank.

I'm going to slip on my CFO hat (full of money) for a moment, Abundant B. Because nothing bothers me more than when women ignore their numbers, cross their fingers, and hope profit will just magically appear.

Yes, your thoughts, energy, and alignment will absolutely bring money to you. But then what? You need to hold on to some of that money so you can actually grow your wealth and step into true financial independence. Attracting it is only part of the story. The other part is creating a money machine that supports you for the long run.

I want you to be profitable for so many reasons. First, because profit means you actually get to keep the money you've worked so hard to make and attract. Second, profitability fuels your confidence. It creates the energy and momentum to think bigger, dream bolder, and keep building. Without profit, business can feel like a never-ending rollercoaster of feast or famine. And as part of my personal mission, I want to empower women to break that cycle and finally feel at home with their finances. That's why I wrote my first book, *She Grows Rich: How to Become a Financial Powerhouse.*

Most women avoid their numbers, especially their business numbers. One of my clients, Sheila, was a phenomenal singer. Truly, she had the voice of an angel. She knew her passion, she was living her dream, but she wasn't keeping any of it. In fact, after twenty years as an entertainer, she had operated at a loss every single year. Her belief was, "That's just what singers do."

She was blessed with a supportive husband who provided for their family, but when she came to me, she was exhausted from losing money and from life on the road. And desperate to be home more for her son.

The truth? She was terrified of looking at her numbers. She could barely open them with me, because she thought they would reveal something shameful. She knew she wasn't profitable. She had been pulling from personal money just to keep her business afloat, but she didn't know why.

Together, we shifted two things. First, we reviewed every gig, looking at revenue and expenses to determine profitability. We discovered one that wasn't profitable but consistently opened doors for other high-paying opportunities, so we kept it. Every other gig became a numbers-first decision. If it wasn't profitable, it was a no. For the first time, Sheila realized she had permission to say no to what didn't serve her. That alone was liberating.

Second, we created a new revenue stream she could do from home. She mentored other women who wanted to follow in her footsteps. She quickly packaged it, sold it out, and within weeks had made enough to cover the cost of my coaching and more. That year marked the first in her career when she turned a profit.

The fundamental transformation wasn't just financial. It was in her identity. She shifted from hobbyist to businesswoman. From struggling entertainer to financially empowered entrepreneur. She finally saw that she could be profitable, that she could create stability and abundance for her family, and most importantly, that she was worthy of it.

And we did one more thing. We separated her personal and business finances. I see women skip this step all the time, and it's a big pitfall. If you've set up an LLC to protect your personal assets, but you're co-mingling personal and business funds, you've likely just undone that protection. I'm not a lawyer, so I won't give you legal advice, but common sense tells us that if you blur those lines, the protection won't hold up.

I can't tell you how many times I've heard women say, "I'm bad with money." "I'm bad at numbers," or "I was never good at math." Especially my creative clients—designers, coaches, artists, performers. The story is often, "I'm not a numbers person."

But you don't need to be a numbers person to run a profitable business. You don't need to love math. You don't need to be the kind of person who geeks out over spreadsheets. You just need to be willing to look. To notice. To pay attention. To take action. **Because money clarity isn't about math, it's about empowerment.**

It's about confidence. It's about deciding that your money matters enough to give it your attention.

I've worked with countless women who carried the belief that they were "bad with numbers." Do you know what always happens? Once we sit down together and look at their financials, they realize it's nowhere near as scary as they imagined. They actually feel relief. The numbers start to tell them a story, and suddenly, they can see where their business is leaking money and where it's overflowing. And from there, they finally feel in control.

And let's be real for a second: an Abundant B doesn't shove receipts in a shoebox and hope her accountant figures it out (I see you). She doesn't swipe her business card at Target and call it "marketing." She doesn't avoid her bank account until the credit card company calls.

An Abundant B partners with her money. She chooses clarity over confusion. She knows that clarity creates confidence, and confidence creates cash. Ka-ching!

Revenue might make you look successful from the outside, but profit is what makes you feel powerful on the inside.

Profit is what allows you to exhale. It's what gives you choices, confidence, and the freedom to actually enjoy the life and business you've worked so hard to create. And most of all, be proud of it.

Trust me, your numbers are not the enemy. Once you understand them, they actually give you so much clarity and confidence that you'll learn to love them. They reflect what's flowing in and what's flowing out, nothing more, nothing less. Just like a mirror in your bathroom isn't judging you for bedhead, your Profit and Loss statement isn't judging you either. It's simply showing you where you are so you can decide where you want to go next. It's that simple.

Money deserves your time and energy if you want more of it.

Every woman deserves to understand her business finances without overwhelm, and to feel confident making decisions that actually grow her wealth.

I've worked with plenty of business owners in my career as a CFO. And you know what I've noticed? The ones who grow and expand are the ones who know their numbers and look at them every single month. They don't guess, they don't hope, they know. They know the exact number they need to hit to keep the lights on, and they know that once they pass it, everything after that is all profit. And it fuels them to go further.

It's a powerful number to have at your fingertips. I call it your monthly "nut." When you know it, you stop running your business on vibes and start running it with clarity. Remember: clarity gives you confidence. And confidence creates more cash.

Numbers don't have to feel heavy or confusing. Once you see how simple it can be, you'll never want to go back to ignoring them. That's why I created a course called Profitable Business Academy, because every woman deserves to understand her business finances without overwhelm and to feel confident making decisions that actually grow her wealth.

An Abundant B understands that every dollar she keeps fuels her confidence, her energy, her future abundance, and keeps that money machine running strong.

So here's your move, Abundant B. Stop hiding from your numbers. They're not here to scare you; they're here to guide you. Pull them up, even if it feels uncomfortable, and take a high-level look. Where is money flowing in? Where is it flowing out?

You don't need to be a CPA or spend hours in spreadsheets. But you do need to know a few simple truths about your business:

What are you spending each month to run it?

What's the minimum revenue you need to bring in to cover that?

And what's the revenue goal you want to hit to grow your wealth and fund your abundant life?

To get started, review the last 6–12 months (preferably 12) of your business numbers and write down the following:

Your average monthly revenue

Where are you spending most of your money

And ask yourself: Does this spending align with my goals and the way I actually want to use my income?

Now let's talk about your monthly nut. This is just a simple way of saying the minimum amount of money you need to bring in every month to cover your expenses. Here's how to find it: add up your total business expenses for the last 6–12 months, then divide by the number of months. That gives you your average.

To make it even simpler, group your expenses into a few broad categories so you can see where your money is actually going. For example:

- Professional development (courses, programs, masterminds, coaching, mentors)
- Marketing and advertising
- Travel
- Office expenses
- Team
- Software
- Dues and subscriptions

For example:

If your business expenses were $60,000 over the last 12 months, your monthly nut is $5,000. That means the first $5,000 you bring in each month covers your costs. Anything beyond that is profit.

If your expenses average $8,000 a month and you consistently bring in $12,000, then you know you're running at about $4,000 in profit. That's clarity.

And here's the reframe: when you sit down with your numbers, don't approach it as punishment. Approach it as pride. Every dollar that moves through your business is proof that you are creating something real. That you are a woman building wealth and impact. Instead of shaming yourself for what you think you've done "wrong," celebrate yourself for the courage to look, learn, and lead.

Now, I know this is a manifestation book, and here I am putting on my CFO hat. Let me pause and say, I get it. Talking about numbers might feel less "woo" than the rest of this journey. But let me tell you why this matters. Clarity with your finances can shift your manifesting more than almost anything else. When you know exactly what you need and what you desire, you can align your thoughts, energy, and actions with so much more power. With clarity comes so much power!

The secret most manifestation gurus miss is this:

Money loves a purpose.

It's not enough to know what's coming in and going out; you need to tell your money what you want it to do. When money has direction, it flows faster. When it has a purpose, it multiplies.

Think about it, if money doesn't have a job, it slips away. But when you decide, "This money is paying my team, this money is going into investments or savings, this money is funding my dream house or creating generational wealth," you give money a reason to show up.

This is the foundation for the Financial Abundance Audio you'll create in the next chapter. Because you can't design your dream life if you don't know what you're building on or what you want the money to do once it arrives.

When you know your numbers and give your money purpose, you feed your money machine. You give it the fuel to grow, expand, and create abundance that lasts. And most of all, you get to be proud of it.

That's it. Simple. No overwhelm, simply knowing the number that keeps the lights on and the business running. Once you know your nut, you can breathe easier, because you'll see the exact moment you cross into profit.

As women, we have the privilege of creating businesses today. That wasn't always the case. Just a few generations ago, women couldn't open bank accounts without a husband's signature. They couldn't get business loans. They were often expected to stay small, to stay home, to stay quiet.

We are the first generation who gets to do this differently. Who gets to build wealth in our own names. Who gets to use our voices, our brilliance, and our businesses to create freedom. That's why it matters so much that you not only start a business, but build a profitable one.

Profit isn't just about money; it's about power, choice, and legacy.

You get to take ownership, Abundant B. Build the best damn profitable business you can. Not just for yourself, but for everyone who comes after you. Every time you raise your prices, say no to a non-profitable gig, or proudly review your numbers, you are breaking cycles. You are rewriting history.

When you rise, you don't just rise for yourself; you rise for every woman watching. For your daughters, your sisters, your cousins, and friends. For the women who look at you and think, "If she can do it, maybe I can too." And more women are looking at you than you'll ever know.

Profit gives you more than cash in the bank. It gives you the power to model what's possible. To show other women how it's done. To create a ripple effect that outlives you.

This is the real work of an Abundant B. Yes, to manifest, yes, to attract, but also to own, to lead, and to create profit. Because when you profit, you prove that women's businesses are not hobbies, they're legacies.

And I want you to see what this looks like in real life. One of my coaching clients, Kelly, is a perfect example. She's a luxury interior designer with almost 20 years in business. She built a beautiful reputation, but behind the scenes, she didn't feel confident in her numbers. Like so many women entrepreneurs, she focused on doing incredible work for her clients while avoiding the financial side of the business. She didn't know how to read or understand her financial statements—what they meant or how to use them. She was running a seven-figure business that wasn't profitable, and she couldn't figure out why.

When we worked together, the first thing we did was bring clarity to her numbers: her revenue, her expenses, her profitability. And that clarity changed everything. Suddenly, she wasn't making decisions in the dark. She could see exactly what was working, what wasn't, and how to move forward with confidence.

We made a couple of simple shifts in her team that at first cost her a little more money, but then her business exploded. Her revenue practically doubled. She went from $1M to $1.7M, and most of that increase went straight to her bottom line as profit. The shifts in her team, including replacing a departing junior designer with someone more senior, only cost an additional $10,000 per year. Still, by putting the right people in the right positions, her business skyrocketed in just a few months. That's the power of knowing and using your numbers.

With that foundation, Kelly was able to scale her business without the constant stress of "I have no money to pay my team." She stepped fully into her role as CEO, not just as a designer, and her confidence grew right alongside her profits. And her energy and enthusiasm for her business expanded tenfold.

When she first came to me, Kelly wasn't even sure she wanted to keep her business going. That's the toll of running without profit. It drains you, exhausts you, and makes you question whether it's worth it at all. But with clarity and a willingness to own her numbers, she not only kept her business, but she also completely transformed it.

And this is what I want for you, Abundant B. To stop second-guessing yourself. To stop hiding from your numbers. To take back your power, step fully into your CEO role, and build the kind of profitable business that lights you up instead of drains you.

Because clarity creates confidence. Confidence creates cash. And cash creates choices.

And those choices? They are the building blocks of your abundant life.

Now, you're ready for the next step. In the next chapter, you'll create your Financial Abundance Audio, your personal blueprint for calling in exactly what you desire. This isn't just about setting goals; it's about rewiring your subconscious, so abundance flows to you on autopilot. You'll take the clarity you've just created and turn it into a vision so magnetic, the Universe can't help but respond.

Are you ready?!

chapter seven

FINANCIAL ABUNDANCE ON AUTOPILOT

I still remember the first time I created what my coach called a "Brain Prime." She used that term for a technique designed to reprogram your subconscious to achieve your goals. It involves creating an audio recording in your own voice detailing the outcome you want to create. Personally, I'm not a huge fan of the term, which is why you'll hear me use it a little differently. But back then, it was new to me.

At the time, I was standing at a crossroad. I desperately wanted to become a coach, but my mind was on repeat with one loud, limiting thought: Who am I to be a coach? That single thought hijacked everything. Remember the TEAR model from Chapter 3? That was playing out in real time.

Thought was Who am I to be a coach?

Emotion it triggered was fear.

Action (or in this case, inaction) was paralysis. I didn't put myself out there, didn't call myself a coach, didn't take the first step.

Result was exactly what you'd expect. Nothing changed.

Then I recorded my first brain prime. In this audio recording, I told myself I was a powerful coach who created transformations for her clients. As instructed, I listened to this recording every morning. Then all of a sudden, something shifted. Instead of replaying fear, my subconscious began feeding me new instructions. I started showing up differently, thinking of myself as a coach, taking action without overthinking. What had once felt impossible suddenly felt natural. It was so crazy, and so easy, that I knew I had stumbled onto something powerful. That one experience is what ultimately led me to become a certified NeuroCoach, so I could study and master this system for myself and for others.

The full NeuroCoaching process is deep. It's a twelve-week journey of one-on-one coaching, uncovering limiting beliefs, rewriting them, and then building a highly customized brain prime. It's very powerful, but it's also a big investment of time and energy.

What I discovered along the way, though, is that there's a shortcut. I realized I could take the essence of that system and use it to create a streamlined version that reprograms your subconscious faster, specifically, to bring in financial abundance on autopilot. I call it Financial Abundance Audio. That's exactly what this chapter is about.

The first time I recorded this Financial Abundance Audio for myself, I told myself things like, "Money comes to me with ease, grace, and in ever-increasing amounts from multiple sources. Every dollar I receive is infused with purpose and flows into my world in ways that support my highest good. I am here to serve."

In just two and a half weeks, I manifested almost two times what my monthly goal was at the time. Now, let me be clear, it doesn't always happen that quickly. Neuroscience tells us it takes about ten weeks of consistent daily listening for new programming to fully take root in our subconscious. But when you combine this tool with the manifestation practices I've already shared in this book, it becomes a superpower. It's like strapping a rocket booster onto your intentions.

And in this chapter, I'm going to hand you that rocket booster.

Abundant B, your subconscious isn't some fluffy concept. It's biology. It's the wiring in your brain that decides whether you stay stuck in the same old patterns or step into the woman who creates abundance on autopilot. And when you learn how to work with it, everything changes. Buckle up, Buttercup, because this is where it gets really interesting.

Your brain has billions of neurons, and they're constantly sparking and connecting. Every time you think a thought, whether it's "I'll never figure this out" or "I'm magnetic and money flows to me," you're strengthening a pathway. The more you repeat it, the stronger it gets. The ones you stop using? They fade away. Neuroscientists call this synaptic pruning. I call it proof that you can change your story any time you decide to.

That's why one pep talk, one journal entry, or one good day doesn't rewire you. Your brain doesn't flip that fast. But when you come back to the same abundant thought over and over again, through your audio, you're training it to become your new default. You're teaching your subconscious, "This is who I am now, this is what matters, this is my new normal." And eventually your brain listens. It has to.

As I mentioned, it takes about ten weeks of daily listening for those new pathways to take over. Not because ten is magical, but because that's how long it takes for the old story to weaken and the new one to take hold. It's science. Think of it like building muscle. You wouldn't expect abs after one workout, but show up consistently, and the results are undeniable. Your audio is the gym session for your wealthy identity.

And this is the fun part: your brain is always scanning for proof of whatever you feed it. Remember the filter in your head called the Reticular Activating System, or RAS, that I mentioned in Chapter 3? It decides what gets your attention and what gets ignored. When you tell it every day through your audio, "I am abundant, clients love to work with me, money flows easily," your RAS goes out into the world and looks for evidence of exactly that. Suddenly, you see opportunities you used to scroll past. A client inquiry lands in your inbox "out of nowhere." The right person introduces themselves at the exact right time. That's not random; that's your brain doing its job with new instructions.

Timing makes it even more powerful. First thing in the morning, before bed, or while you're walking are the best windows because your subconscious is wide open. Your guard is down. In those states, your brain takes what you tell it and treats it as fact.

And don't underestimate the power of your own voice. Hearing yourself say, "I am abundant, I am magnetic, money flows to me with ease," hits differently than reading it in a book or hearing it from someone else. Your brain tags your own voice as more important. It's like your subconscious saying, "Oh, she means this."

My client, Hailey, actually hates to hear her own voice, so she put her Financial Abundance Audio in written format and keeps it on her desk to read often. It takes a little more work to do it this way, but if you're like her and the sound of your own voice feels uncomfortable, know that there are options. The key is consistency. Whether you're listening or reading, the repetition is what rewires your brain.

The more emotion you bring in, the faster it sticks. If you just drone through the words, your brain files it away as background noise. But if you close your eyes, smile, and feel the gratitude of already living it, your nervous system lights up. Your brain marks it as important, and the new wiring locks in deeper.

This is why athletes visually rehearse winning before they compete, why musicians practice songs in their heads before they ever touch an instrument. The brain doesn't know the difference between imagining and doing. Your Financial Abundance Audio is you rehearsing your abundant life until it becomes the only outcome your brain will accept.

So no, this isn't busy work. It's not a cute routine. It's science. It's your subconscious clearing out the old junk, wiring in new patterns, and filtering the world to match. When you stay consistent, your reality doesn't just shift, it completely transforms. It's not magic. It's science.

Now that you know why this works, let's talk about how to actually create your own Financial Abundance Audio. You're going to take everything we just covered and turn it into a daily ritual that puts your financial goals on autopilot.

STEP 1: CHOOSE YOUR MONTHLY NUMBER

Here's where most women trip themselves up. They either pick a number so small it doesn't stretch them, or they choose something so big their subconscious calls bullshit and shuts it down. We're going to find the sweet spot. A number that feels exciting and expansive but still believable to your nervous system.

And here's the important part: release the "how" it comes in. It doesn't have to all come from your business. Abundance isn't limited to invoices and sales. It can flow through unexpected ways, such as refunds, surprise checks, gifts, investments, and opportunities you never saw coming. When I manifested $29,000 in two and a half weeks, none of it came from my business. Which honestly blew my mind. It was all unexpected, personal money. And that experience reminded me of one of the hardest but most powerful parts of manifesting, which is letting go of the "how."

Your job isn't to control every step or force the exact path the money has to take. Your job is to choose the number, declare it, and trust your brain and the Universe to figure out the details. That's the fun part and also what most people find very difficult. They think they need to know exactly where it's coming from, but that only puts pressure on the process. When you release the "how," you stay open to receiving in ways your logical mind could never have predicted.

Think about the next 90 days. Not "someday," not "five years from now." I want you to see success fast so you will continue using this process to dream bigger and bigger. If you're torn between two numbers, choose the one that makes you light up with excitement and a tiny edge of discomfort. That little flutter in your heart of "Can I really do this?" is the sweet spot. A number that excites you and motivates you to move forward.

And one more thing, please choose one number to start, not a range. Your brain doesn't do well with fuzzy math. If you tell it "between $10,000 and $15,000," it has no idea where to land. But if you declare, "$15,000 flows to me every month," it has a clear target. Think of it like putting an address into your GPS. You don't just type "somewhere in New York City" and expect your car to take you to the right spot. You punch in the exact destination. Same with your subconscious, it needs precision.

Grab your journal and write down the number you want to see coming into your bank account each month. Feel into it, make sure it's the right number for you before we move on. This is the first building block of your Financial Abundance Audio. And don't worry if you're not sure exactly what to say yet, I'll be giving you a script you can fill in and record as your Financial Abundance Audio.

STEP 2: GIVE YOUR MONEY A MISSION

Money loves a mission, but if you don't give it direction, it tends to disappear. Think of it like a team member. If you don't tell them what to do, they'll wander around aimlessly or focus on the wrong things. But when you give clear instructions, money knows exactly where to go and how to serve you. Also, the universe knows exactly why to bring you this money. It wants to make you happy, and if you are clear as to how you want to use this money to make yourself happy, it will oblige.

Most people make this mistake, including myself, before I knew this trick. They set a big income goal, but they never decide what that money is for. It's like telling the Universe you want more money but not explaining why. You want the power of the Universe behind you. It wants you to do good things with the money, so show it what you will be doing. After all, we can't take the money with us. We get to support ourselves, our family, our team, and their families, future generations, charities, and causes. When you pre-decide where your money will flow, and flow with love, you give your subconscious a powerful reason to go out and make it happen.

This step is all about assigning your chosen number a mission. Round your number to the nearest $500 (because your brain loves simplicity, and so do I) and decide where it will go across your business and life. Don't overthink this. The goal is to create a plan that excites you and makes your brain say, "Yes, this feels good, this feels doable." It just needs to add up to the number you chose in step 1.

For example, let's say your monthly number from step one is $15,000. You might split it like this:

Business:

- $1,000–Team
- $1,000–Software & Systems
- $1,000–Coaching/Professional Development
- $1,000–Debt Paydown
- $1,000–Travel

Personal:

- $3,500–Mortgage/Rent/Taxes
- $500–Self-Care (gym, massages, hair, nails)
- $500–Car payment
- $1,000 Vacation/Travel
- $2,500–Spending (groceries, eating out, pets, supplies, charity)
- $1,000–Savings/Investing (retirement, college, general)

When you see your money divided up like this, it becomes real. It's no longer just a number on paper; it's the house you live in, the self-care that nourishes you, the vacations you take, the team that supports your business. Every dollar is aligned and fueling your greater mission.

Here's the magic — your subconscious gets fired up when it has a mission. It's not motivated by "$15,000" as an abstract number. But when it sees that this money means your mortgage is paid, your savings are growing, your family vacation is booked, and your business is thriving, it locks onto the vision. Your brain says, "Oh, this matters," and it goes to work spotting opportunities and pulling in evidence to make it real.

And don't worry if your allocations aren't perfect. This isn't about math being exact down to the penny; it's about creating alignment. The point is to connect your number to a life that excites you, because emotion is what programs your subconscious.

Now take a moment to write out your own breakdown. Assign every dollar of your monthly number to something that matters to you. The more specific you are, the stronger the wiring becomes. And remember, you're the CEO here. You get to decide how your money supports your life and business without judgment or guilt.

This step turns your income goal into a mission. And when money has a mission, it knows exactly where to go.

STEP 3: CREATE YOUR FINANCIAL ABUNDANCE SCRIPT

Now that you've chosen your number and given your money a mission, it's time to bring it all to life with your Financial Abundance Audio Script. This is the heart of your audio, the words you'll record and listen to daily for the next 10 weeks. Keep it short enough that you can read it in about four to five minutes. That's the sweet spot. This way, it won't take too much of your time each day, and it will be easy to stay consistent with listening daily.

And, Abundant B, your brain doesn't process negatives. If I tell you not to think of a red car, what pops into your mind first? A bright red car. That's how the subconscious works. It doesn't hear the word "not," it just sees the picture. That's why every word in your script needs to be framed in the positive.

And it also needs to sound like you. This isn't about reciting my words or repeating affirmations that don't feel aligned. If something doesn't resonate, change it. Swap out a word, choose the option that feels best. I'll give you some options in parentheses. You can use them as-is or fill in your own. The more the script sounds like your voice, the faster your subconscious will accept it as truth. It will only work if you and your subconscious believe it is true and possible. And be specific. The more detail you give your subconscious— the mortgage paid, the team you hire, the vacation you take—the easier it is for your brain to lock onto the vision.

The key is to keep it positive, keep it exciting, and keep it fueling your desire. You want every line to excite you, to make you nod your head and feel that "yes" in your body. That's when you know you've nailed it. And most of all, have fun with it. This isn't about pressure. iIt's about creating words that make you feel grateful and inspired every time you hear them. I want you to LOVE listening to this every day as my clients do.

Now it's your turn. Here's your Financial Abundance Audio Script template. Make it yours, fill it with your truth, and let it fill you with anticipation every single day. I can't wait for you to create the abundance and life of your dreams!

If you'd like a clean copy of the following script in a Google Doc format, just scan the QR code on this page, and it will be ready for you.

FINANCIAL ABUNDANCE AUDIO SCRIPT

Of course, $______________ (insert $ from step 1) flows effortlessly into my bank accounts every month. This is my baseline, my standard, my new normal. And the truth is, I am capable of even more.

I believe this amount is fully possible for me because ______________ (Choose one - God/Universe) hasn't brought me here to leave me here, my purpose is divinely connected, I was born to have this impact and abundance.

Money comes to me with ease, grace, and in ever-increasing amounts from multiple sources. The Universe [or God] is always conspiring in my favor, aligning the right opportunities, the perfect clients, and the most abundant experiences to support my growth and impact.

I trust this because what is meant for me will never pass me by. I can feel the divine guidance that brought me here, and I know the Universe [or God] is bringing me even more than I can imagine.

I desire this money because I am meant for it. It supports my beautiful, abundant life ______________ (list a few general personal things from step 2 this money will support, such as home, self-care, savings, investments, experiences, etc.). *Every dollar I receive is infused with a mission and purpose and flows into my world in a way that supports my highest good. I easily cover ______________* (list more specific expenses, such as mortgage, rent, student loans, gym, travel, team, business growth, etc. from step 2). *Every time I spend money, I feel grateful, expansive, and deeply supported, knowing that even more is on its way to me.*

My business is thriving. I have all the money I need to invest in my growth, my marketing, my ______________(list any business expenses, team members or resources that support your success, such as virtual assistant, mentor, courses, or software from Step 2), *and the systems that allow my business to run* *smoothly and powerfully. Every dollar I invest comes back to me tenfold, effortlessly.*

I am here to serve. Selling is serving. I sell from my heart and soul, knowing that my work transforms lives in profound and lasting ways. I magnetize the most aligned, ready, and excited clients into my world. (Describe how you want clients to find you: "Clients reach out to me daily, eager to work with me. The right people always find me at the perfect time.")

My _________________ (insert courses, programs, or business offerings) *is* (are) *thriving. It (they) is* (are) *a massive success, selling effortlessly because it is exactly what my clients need. I look forward to serving the brilliant people I attract each month, watching them transform, grow, and step into their power. Every time someone* _________________ (joins one of my programs, starts working with me, purchases my _________________), *it is a celebration, a confirmation that I am on the right path, that my work is divinely guided and deeply needed.*

I am a beautiful blend of heart, soul, and unwavering confidence. I deeply want people to win, to succeed, to thrive. I am a total badass with real, deep knowledge and expertise that creates results. My clients love working with me. They experience radical transformations. They become more/better _________________, *more/better* _________________, *and more/better* _________________ (examples: more confident leaders, better communicators, stronger decision-makers) *with every interaction we have.*

Money loves me. It flows to me in bigger and bigger amounts, through expected and unexpected avenues. I am financially independent. I have more than enough. I overflow. My wealth is ever-expanding. Every dollar I receive is a reminder of the massive impact I am making. I am worthy. I am ready. It is done. And so it is.

STEP 4: RECORD & REPROGRAM

Pull out your phone and record a quick note in Voice Memos. Nothing fancy. No editing required. Your voice is the most powerful tool you have. When your subconscious hears you declaring these words, it accepts them far faster than if you were listening to someone else.

Your script should only be around 4–5 minutes long. That's intentional. It needs to be short enough that you'll actually listen to it daily, but long enough to saturate your subconscious with your new beliefs. Fifteen minutes a day, three listens, is all it takes. That's 70 days, or 10 weeks, to literally rewire your brain.

Repetition is what creates new neural pathways. The more often you listen, the stronger those pathways become, until your new beliefs feel like second nature. It's like lifting weights for your brain. You don't get stronger by doing one workout, you get stronger by showing up consistently for many days.

The best times to listen are when your subconscious is most open:

First thing in the morning (before the world floods in with emails and notifications).

Last thing before you go to sleep (your brain drifts into theta state, the gateway to your subconscious).

While you're walking or moving rhythmically (this puts your brain in a relaxed, open state).

Personally, I walk first thing every morning and listen to mine. There's something powerful about pairing movement with your audio. Your body gets into flow, your mind relaxes, and your subconscious is wide open to receive.

When should you not listen? Don't play your audio when your mind is racing with a million things, when you're distracted, or when you're trying to multitask. Your subconscious won't absorb it the same way if you're focused elsewhere. That's why walking works so well. It's rhythmic, repetitive, and almost mindless. Those kinds of movements put your brain into a relaxed state, the exact state where your subconscious is open and ready to be reprogrammed.

And here's the key: don't just let the words wash over you, focus on them. Visualize this new life. Feel it. Let yourself imagine the money flowing in, the clients showing up, the team supporting you, the joy of spending from overflow. Your subconscious doesn't know the difference between a vividly imagined future and reality. It just takes the input and runs with it.

So yes, this might feel simple. Just listening to your own voice every day? But remember what we discussed earlier, this isn't busy work. It's science. It's you rewiring your brain, pruning away the old pathways of lack and wiring in new patterns of abundance. Stick with it, and it won't just shift your mindset. It will change what you see, what you attract, what you create, and your life.

Commit to this practice for 10 weeks, no excuses. Show up for yourself like you would for your biggest client or your closest friend. If you do, I promise, you'll look back at the end of these 70 days and barely recognize the woman you've become. You'll be your next-level self—confident, magnetic, and abundant on autopilot. And if you miss a day, don't fret. Just tack an extra day onto the end. If you miss more than one day, or even a week, keep going. Don't give up. Keep listening. Add some extra weeks if you need to, or restart if that feels better. The key is completing 70 days.. Even if it hasn't shown up yet, your brain is diligently at work aligning everything for you to achieve it and receive it.

Even if this feels new or a little uncomfortable right now, remember who you are. You're an Abundant B. You've walked through harder things than this, and you've always found a way. This is no different. Every time you hit play on that audio, you're declaring to the Universe, "Watch me." You're building momentum, wiring in power, and stepping into the version of you who doesn't just hope for abundance; she creates it on autopilot.

And to show you how powerful this gets when you lean in, let me introduce you to Amie. When she first came into my Money Mindset & Manifestation Accelerator, she had been an entrepreneur for years. For the last year, her revenue had hovered around $10K a month. Steady, but stuck. And here's the kicker, she was afraid of hitting $20K months again. Why? Because the last time she'd reached that level, it nearly broke her. It came at the cost of long hours, missed family moments, and the sinking feeling that success meant sacrificing her health and her time with her daughters.

Deep down, she wanted more. She craved consistent $20K months that felt sustainable. She wanted to grow her income while still being present for her family and her own well-being. But the belief she kept bumping into was, "If I grow, I'll lose myself and my family in the process."

That belief had her holding back. She told me she would even lower her income goals on purpose just to avoid disappointment. It felt safer to stay small than to aim higher and risk reliving the burnout she had experienced before. Sound familiar?

The shift happened when Amie decided to give herself fully to this process. She went all in with her Financial Abundance Audio. She let herself believe that money could flow from multiple places, not just her business, and that she didn't have to work harder or sacrifice her values to receive it. And whenever doubt crept in, she paired her audio with EFT tapping. Tapping gave her body the signal of safety her subconscious needed, calming the old fear of burnout so she could fully anchor into her new belief. We'll be talking about EFT tapping next and how you can weave that into your practice.

And the results? Within her first two months in the Accelerator, she didn't just hit her $20K per month goal, she blew past it. By month two, she had already brought in $27K, and not all of it from her business. Just as I taught you in Step 1, Amie realized she could let go of the how and stay open to money flowing in from all sources. That awareness alone shifted her entire relationship with abundance.

But here's what I love most. It wasn't just about the money. Amie told me she feels more present with her family, more energized in her business, and more grateful in the little everyday moments of life. She still works about 30 hours a week, but now she does it with ease and joy instead of hustle and sacrifice. Her income is consistent, her business is thriving, and she gets to love her life at the same time.

That's the power of this work. It's not just numbers in your bank account; it's about becoming the woman who attracts, receives, and enjoys abundance on every level. And as Amie's story shows, pairing your Financial Abundance Audio with tapping can be the bridge that keeps your subconscious steady and your energy clear while you step into bigger goals.

In the next chapter, we're going to dive into EFT tapping, what it is, why it works, and how to use it alongside your Financial Abundance Audio to release resistance, calm your nervous system, and amplify everything you've just built here. Get ready, Abundant B, because this is where things get even more magical.

chapter eight

TAP INTO YOUR ABUNDANT B POWER

If you remember, back in Chapter 1, I shared how I stumbled into tapping at a time when fear of the unknown was running my life. I had left behind my biggest CFO retainers, and even though I had savings in the bank, my body didn't feel safe. There was a knot in my stomach that wouldn't loosen, a constant hum of anxiety I couldn't escape. Logically, I knew I was okay. But no matter how many times I looked at the numbers, my nervous system didn't believe me.

I admitted my fear of the unknown out loud, words I had rarely spoken to anyone else. The moment I voiced them while tapping through the protocol you'll learn in this chapter, it was like something cracked open.

In that tapping seat, the dots connected. It wasn't just about the money. It was about my body remembering fear from my childhood.

That moment changed everything. Because freedom isn't only about money, it's about releasing the thoughts that keep you trapped. It's about knowing in your bones that you're safe, no matter what's in front of you.

That's the gift tapping gave me. And it's why I became certified in it, so I could bring that same freedom to the women I work with. We all carry fears, stories, and old beliefs that run the show until we meet them head-on. Tapping became my way to meet them, clear them, and create space for abundance to flow in. Since then, I've guided hundreds of women through this exact process, and I've seen the same magic unfold for them, again and again.

What I quickly realized is that the same fear I felt around the unknown is what so many women and many of my clients can sometimes feel around money. I would watch them freeze when it was time to look at their numbers. I'd see the panic in their eyes when cash flow dipped or when it came time to raise their prices. Sometimes their scarcity mindset felt impenetrable, so that no amount of journaling or positive affirmations could get through the wall of fear. And truthfully, it couldn't. Affirmations bounce right off when your nervous system is in fight-or-flight.

That's where tapping changes everything. Instead of trying to push or think your way out of fear, you tap your way through it. It gives the body a way to release the charge so the mind can finally catch up. It's like opening a window in a stuffy room. Suddenly there's space to breathe, space to dream, space to believe that something more is possible. For women who had been stuck in cycles of scarcity, this was the tool that cracked them open.

And here's the best part. You can't do it wrong. Even if you simply follow along with my words, you'll feel a shift. But if you allow yourself to use your own words, like my client, Lily, did, the impact is even more powerful.

When Lily came to work with me, she was frustrated and exhausted. No matter what she did, her income kept bouncing between inconsistent highs and the bare minimum she needed to scrape by. She told me it felt like she was running on a hamster wheel, always moving, never getting anywhere. And underneath it all was fear. Fear that she couldn't sustain her business. Fear that she would never get ahead.

During one of our sessions together, I asked her to rate the intensity of that fear on a scale from one to ten. This is a tool I often use with tapping because it helps us track the emotional charge. Most women I work with come in somewhere between a seven and a ten.

When I asked Lily, she didn't hesitate. "Eight," she said. That's how consuming it felt in her body. So we started tapping. Point by point, she gave herself permission to voice the thoughts she had been holding inside. The doubts, the "what ifs," the worries that kept her awake at night. She wasn't repeating someone else's words; she was finally speaking her own truth.

And then the shift came. Within a few minutes, the fear that had felt like an eight dropped down to a two. Her energy lightened up. I could see it on her face. She looked at me wide-eyed and said she couldn't believe how different she felt in such a short amount of time.

That session didn't just give Lily temporary relief. It unlocked something bigger. For the first time, she stopped obsessing over how the money would come. She loosened her grip, trusted the process, and opened herself to receive. Within weeks, she had tripled her income. Not because she worked harder, but because she finally created space for abundance to flow in.

What happened for Lily isn't unique to her. And the good news is, you can do this for yourself, too.

Here is how it works:

Start by tuning in to what you're feeling and give it a number. Use the same one-to-ten scale I used with Lily. As I mentioned, most women I work with begin somewhere between a seven and a ten. And here's why that matters. If you're an eight (like Lily was) or above, you're in full fight-or-flight mode. Your nervous system has taken over. Nothing you try to do in that state will actually make you feel better, and you certainly won't be able to come up with fresh ideas or solutions. That's why tapping is such a game-changer. It calms the body so the mind can finally work for you again.

Flip to the tapping diagram on the next page. You'll see the sequence and points we use for tapping. Starting on the side of the hand, then moving through the points on the face, collarbone, underarm, and finally the top of the head. Use two to four fingers on the side of either hand. And you'll only use the side of the hand for the first tapping round. This is when we acknowledge your feelings and let your body know it's totally fine to feel this way. Then use two fingers and tap around seven times on each point. It doesn't matter which side of the face you use, either. Don't overthink it.

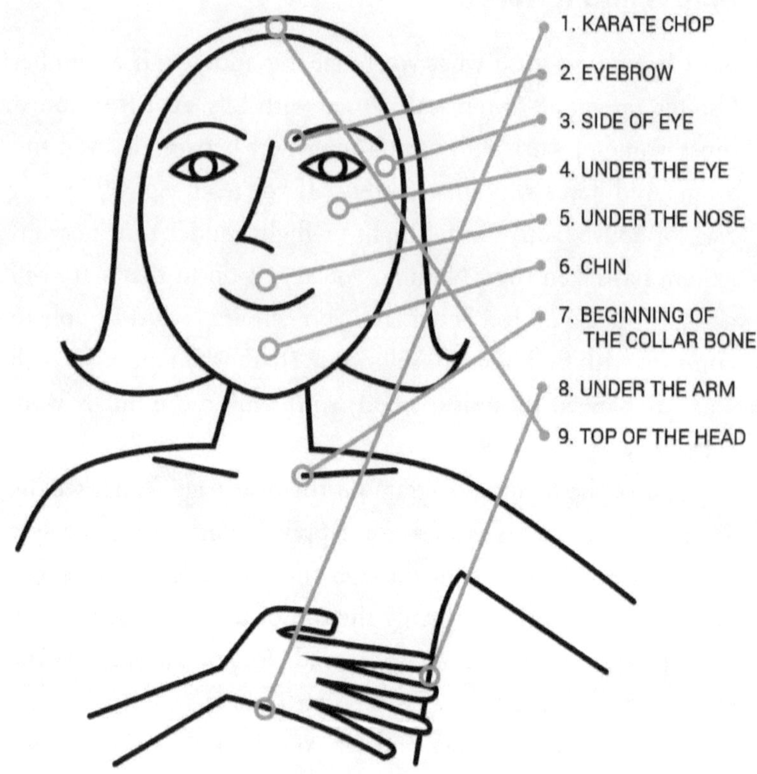

Here are the main tapping points and abbreviations we'll be using:

- *KC = Karate Chop (side of the hand)*
- *EB = Eyebrow (inner edge)*
- *SE = Side of Eye (temple)*
- *UE = Under Eye (cheekbone)*
- *UN = Under Nose*
- *CH = Chin (crease between lip and chin)*
- *CB = Collarbone (just below)*
- *UA = Under Arm (about 4 inches below armpit, bra line)*
- *TH = Top of Head (center)*

In the tapping scripts below, I use these two-letter abbreviations to guide you. That way, you can follow along quickly and easily.

Let's try one together.

Inside the book portal, I've included a video of the following script so you can follow along.

So many of my clients have carried the belief that slowing down means money will stop. Tapping through the following script has been the key to rewriting it.

This script works with a belief that almost every woman entrepreneur has bumped into at some point: I have to constantly hustle and work hard to make money.

TAPPING SCRIPT: I HAVE TO CONSTANTLY HUSTLE AND WORK HARD TO MAKE MONEY

Before we start, rate the intensity of this belief right now on a scale from 1–10. (10 = it feels completely true, 1 = it barely feels true.)

We'll check in after each round to see how it shifts.

Round 1–Negative (KC to TH)

- KC: Even though I believe I have to hustle constantly to make money, I deeply love and accept myself.
- KC: Even though I think if I slow down, the money will stop, I choose to honor how I've been feeling.
- EB: I have to keep working, or the money won't come.
- SE: If I stop hustling, I'll lose it all.
- UE: I've been told my whole life that hard work is the only way.
- UN: It feels unsafe to rest.
- CH: I've linked my worth to how much I do.
- CB: If I'm not busy, I feel guilty.
- UA: I'm afraid to let go of the hustle.
- TH: This belief feels so real in my body.

→ Take a deep breath. Now rate the intensity again (1–10). Notice if anything shifted, even slightly.

If your number shifted down at all, that's proof your body is releasing the charge.

Round 2–Neutral (EB to TH)

- EB: What if money could come without constant grind?
- SE: What if I could take a breath and still be supported?
- UE: Maybe ease could bring in more than hustle ever did.
- UN: Maybe I don't have to earn abundance through exhaustion.
- CH: I'm curious about what it could feel like to slow down.
- CB: I'm open to exploring a different way of working.

- UA: It might be safe to rest and still receive.
- TH: I'm allowing the possibility that money can flow with ease.

→ Deep breath. Now rate the intensity again (1–10).

If your number dropped, even a little, it means your nervous system is already calming and creating space for new possibilities.

Round 3–Positive (EB to TH)

- EB: I choose to believe money can flow with ease.
- SE: I can work smart, not just hard.
- UE: My energy and creativity are my greatest assets.
- UN: I am worthy of money even when I rest.
- CH: Abundance doesn't require burnout.
- CB: I attract wealth through joy, alignment, and inspired action.
- UA: I trust that opportunities arrive at the perfect time.
- TH: I now create money in ways that feel light, spacious, and free.

→ Deep breath. Now rate the intensity again (1–10).

Pay attention to any decrease in intensity. That's proof your energy is shifting and the belief is losing its grip. If you're under a three, you've moved through it. If you're still above a three, feel free to move through rounds two and three again.

Know that tapping will never hurt you. If this belief isn't something you carry, it won't create it. The only thing tapping can do is relax you and bring you back into balance.

Now, just to be clear, the script you just tapped through isn't Lily's. Her breakthrough came from a tapping sequence that was specific to her fears and the exact words she was carrying. That's the beauty of tapping: it's most powerful when you use your own truth.

The script I just shared is fairly universal, and it's one I use often because so many women entrepreneurs carry that belief. But the most life-changing shifts happen when we tap directly on your patterns, your memories, and the beliefs that have been running in the background of your life.

That's why I always encourage my clients, and you, to go deeper. Inside the book portal, you'll find a link to schedule an Abundance Breakthrough Session with me.

This is where we can work through your specific challenges and mindset, and create a tapping sequence designed just for you.

Lily's shift and this script are just two examples of what becomes possible when you clear the charge. And she's not the only one. Let me share another story about Hailey.

Hailey came to me with a different kind of block. Her income had been stuck at the same level for years, no matter how much effort she put in. During one of our group tapping sessions, as she began voicing her feelings, something unexpected rose to the surface.

Through her tears, she blurted out, "I can't make more than my mom." It was like the words had been trapped inside her for decades. She suddenly realized she'd been carrying a subconscious loyalty to her mother, an invisible ceiling that said earning more would mean outshining or betraying her.

This is exactly what tapping does. It not only helps you manage stress, but it also reveals the hidden stories and emotions that have been quietly dictating your life. Hailey's block wasn't about her business model or strategy. It was about guilt. It was about the unspoken belief that wanting more meant leaving her mom behind.

As she tapped through those emotions, the charge began to release. She gave herself permission to love and honor her mom's journey while still creating her own. She realized she didn't have to dim her light to stay connected and that she could rise and still belong.

By the end of the session, she felt lighter, relieved, and more open. And almost instantly, her creativity returned. She began planning a retreat, mapping out her next event, and reigniting the passion she thought she'd lost.

That's the gift of tapping. It doesn't just release fear, it reignites your fire. When the nervous system relaxes, and those old stories lose their grip, your natural energy and inspiration come rushing back in like a dam that's finally broken open, flooding your life with possibility.

Abundant B Prompt

Take a moment to reflect on this: are there any hidden ceilings you've set for yourself? Maybe like Hailey, you've tied your worth or your success to someone else's story. Maybe you've been carrying silent rules about what's "allowed" for you. Write down whatever comes up, no censoring. Let the words spill out, even if they don't fully make sense yet.

Abundant B Mantra

I give myself permission to rise. I can honor the ones who came before me while creating a new path of wealth, freedom, and possibility.

Hailey's story is such a powerful example of how tapping can shatter the hidden ceilings we didn't even know were there. But the shifts don't always show up as big, dramatic breakthroughs. Sometimes they reveal themselves in smaller, everyday ways, like feeling lighter, happier, and more at ease. That's exactly what happened for Autumn.

Autumn described the tapping sessions as "phenomenal." Each time we tapped together, she said it felt like another piece of the wall she had been carrying for years came crumbling down. Not all at once, but layer by layer, fear by fear.

What stood out most was that Autumn didn't just leave tapping in our sessions. She took it with her into her daily life. Whenever fear tried to creep back in like before sending a proposal, before a sales conversation, even in the quiet moments when doubt whispered, she tapped. And every time, she noticed the edge softening.

She told me that sometimes the shifts weren't dramatic, but they were steady. Day by day, she felt lighter, happier, and more at peace. And something else changed, too. She said she was no longer afraid of her numbers. Instead of avoiding them, she began getting curious. What once triggered anxiety became an opportunity to learn and grow.

Tapping is not only a breakthrough in the moment, though those moments are powerful, but it's also a practice you can carry with you anywhere. When scarcity whispers, when self-doubt knocks, when old stories threaten to keep you small, tapping is right there, ready to clear the charge and bring you back to your Abundant B power.

When I think about my own breakthrough with tapping and the transformations I've witnessed with women like Lily, Hailey, and Autumn, one thing is always clear: the fears we carry are never the whole truth. They're old stories, waiting to be released. Tapping gives us a way to move that energy out of the body, to calm the nervous system, and to finally create space for abundance to flow in.

That's why I call it one of the most powerful tools in my Abundant B toolbox. Whether it's breaking through a generational ceiling, letting go of the hustle, or simply finding more peace and curiosity with money, tapping shows us that change doesn't have to be hard. It can be as simple as honoring what's real, tapping through it, and stepping into a lighter, freer version of yourself.

And here's the best part: Once you know how to shift your fear, you're free to embody something bigger. Real abundance isn't measured only by the dollars you hold, but by the identity you embody. Get ready, Abundant B, because next we're stepping into wealth not just as something you have, but as something you are.

chapter nine

THE WOMAN WHO RISES: WEALTH AS IDENTITY

Wealth isn't just about money.

It's not only the number in your bank account or the consistency of your income. It's not even the shiny milestone of tripling your revenue. Those things are real, but they're outcomes. True wealth is identity. It's not what you do, it's who you are.

When you begin to live wealth as your natural state, everything shifts. You stop needing numbers to prove your worth. You start anchoring into sufficiency, expansion, and joy as your baseline. You embody your next-level self before the evidence arrives. And because energy always precedes form, the money and opportunities rise up to meet you.

I learned this on the beautiful, breathtaking cliffs of Greece.

When I said yes to a mastermind retreat, it wasn't the "logical" decision. My mind listed a dozen reasons to say no: the cost, the timing, the logistics, the fact that I could just as easily stay home and "play it safe." But the woman I was becoming knew better. She knew that wealth wasn't safety. Wealth was expanding.

Wealth was saying yes to the experiences that stretched me, lit up my soul, showed me what was possible, and revealed a different way of being. This trip placed me in rooms with women who thought bigger, who embodied abundance in their very presence.

From the first night, Greece began teaching me what it meant to be wealthy.

Maria, a business bestie and travel buddy, and I arrived in Oia with no plans for dinner, only a whispered prayer: "Let God show us the perfect place." I kept pinching myself, not even believing I was really there, that this wasn't just a dream. It was a true vision board image come to life. As we wandered cobblestone streets, I caught sight of a narrow building entrance leading to a long hallway. At the end, a burst of color and light opened into the most breathtaking view of the crisp blue waters of the Aegean Sea. Moments later, a waiter appeared and invited us in. The best table in the house, a table we hadn't reserved, a table that looked like it had been waiting for us, had just opened up. It felt orchestrated by the universe itself.

We sat there in awe, speechless, which is unusual for two Geminis, and nearly in tears. A slight breeze was blowing off the Aegean Sea, scented with a hint of sea salt. The food tasted like heaven. But it wasn't just about the dinner. It was about the receiving. About letting myself be cared for and feeling abundant. About trusting that when I lean back and open my hands, wealth flows in.

The week unfolded like a love letter from the Universe. Sailing on a catamaran past Santorini's red, black, and white beaches, I barely touched my phone. I didn't need to capture it. I lived it. Crystal-clear water sparkled beneath me, the cliffs towered above, and laughter from new friends carried across the boat.

Later in the week, we traveled from Santorini to Amorgos, where the mastermind sessions were being held behind glass walls perched over the sea. I found myself crying tears of gratitude, moved by the depth of connection and support. At night, we laughed, celebrated birthdays, shared meals under string lights, even fed taverna cats (and yes, one adorable donkey who wanted attention too). Joy itself was wealth. Presence was prosperity. I was living an abundant life and was so grateful and blessed. It all felt like a dream.

But the most profound moments came during the mastermind itself.

One morning, the mastermind leader, Sara, led us through a powerful future-self activation. As I closed my eyes, I saw her, the woman I was becoming. She wasn't hustling or hiding. She was visible, magnetic, joyful. She was leading a movement that helped women feel safe and empowered with their finances. When I opened my eyes, I knew I couldn't keep playing small.

Later, I shared my wounds around visibility, the fear of being seen, and the belief that success had to come at a cost with the mastermind group. With Sara's coaching and energetic downloads, something cracked wide open. I left that session no longer doubting if I was ready, but knowing I was already the woman in my vision. I stepped into the identity of Audrey 7.0, confident, unapologetic, embodying wealth as a way of being.

And then came the helicopter.

You see, I didn't leave the island the way I came. While I was supposed to leave by ferry, a series of "coincidences" (that were anything but) aligned so perfectly that I ended up with the most iconic exit I could have imagined. A helicopter!

As the blades began to turn, headset on, wind whipping my hair, I felt something lift inside me, too. Rising above the cliffs, watching Amorgos shrink below me, I knew I wasn't the same woman who had arrived a week earlier. I had stepped into and out of Audrey 7.0 and now flew off that island as Audrey 8.0.

That helicopter wasn't just transportation. It was a declaration. A line in the sand. I was leaving behind the old identity that equated wealth with hustle, overwork, or safety. I was choosing to embody the Abundant B version of me who claims joy, expansion, connection, and divine provision as her birthright.

That's what wealth as a way of being is. It's not about whether the trip "paid for itself" (it did, and more). It's about who I became by saying yes. Wealth is expansion. Wealth is identity. Wealth is joy. It's walking into a restaurant and being handed the perfect table. It's crying tears of gratitude in a glass-walled room over the Aegean. It's boarding a helicopter and knowing, with every fiber of your being, that you will never again go back to playing small. It was time for me to start playing big, and to "Step up, Buttercup."

Wealth is not something you do. It's not about checking the boxes, hitting the goals, or waiting for the numbers to prove you're successful. That's *doing* wealth.

True wealth is about being wealth.

Being wealthy means waking up already anchored in sufficiency. It means carrying yourself with confidence and presence before the results arrive. It means choosing joy, generosity, and expansion as your baseline, instead of scarcity and hustle.

This is where most women get stuck. They think, "When I hit six figures, then I'll feel wealthy." Or "When I pay off debt, then I'll relax." But the truth is, the feeling doesn't come later. You call it in now. You decide who you are before the evidence shows up.

That's why Greece was so transformative for me. Saying yes to that trip was a declaration of identity. Sitting at that divine dinner table was proof that when I lean back and receive, abundance rushes in. Boarding that helicopter was more than travel; it was an embodiment. It was me saying yes to me. That I no longer wait for permission. That I no longer play small. That I am wealth, ready for expansion, and a woman who rises.

Here's the secret: You don't need a mastermind in Amorgos, Greece, or a helicopter exit to practice wealth as a way of being. Although, let's be honest, it was a pretty unforgettable, "Abundant B" way to embody my next-level self. You can start today, in the smallest choices.

When you take a breath before making a decision and ask, "What would my abundant self choose?"

When you savor your coffee in the morning instead of rushing through it.

When you let yourself receive help, compliments, or even the perfect parking spot instead of brushing it off.

When you invest in yourself from trust, not fear.

These are the micro-moments where identity is built. These are the choices that compound into a wealthy way of being.

When I came back from Greece, I didn't want the transformation to stay on the island. I wanted to embody it in my daily life. So I asked myself: What does my abundant self do? How does she live?

The first shift was simple. I started going for weekly massages. I already had a monthly membership and, as it turned out, a stack of credits waiting for me. It didn't cost me anything to make that transition, but it completely changed how I felt. Each massage became a declaration of self-care. It was me saying I am a woman who prioritizes her body, her energy, and her joy.

And then, I started embodying it in my business. I prepared for the next level by hiring an additional team member, promoting my VA into an operations role, and then bringing on a second VA. I put the team in place for the business I was stepping into, not just the business I had. I began acting as if my next level was already here. I built a new Facebook ads funnel, expanded my systems, and created the structure to sustain bigger growth.

In short, I started playing big.

And this is what I want you to see: you don't have to wait. You don't have to wait for the money, the clients, or the milestones. You get to start embodying your wealthy self now.

- Where can you make an easy transition into the life you want, just like I did with those massage credits?
- Where can you upgrade your habits, even in small ways, to reflect your abundant identity?
- Where can you start putting the structures in place for the future you're calling in?

Wealth isn't something you wait for. It's something you become.

Embody it now, and watch your reality rise to meet you.

Abundant B Prompt

Where in your life are you still "taking the ferry" when your soul is calling for the helicopter? What decisions feel safe, logical, or familiar, but aren't aligned with your next-level self? Write down the ways you could start embodying wealth as an identity today, before the external results show up.

For the audio version of the following visualization, please visit the book portal:

ABUNDANT B VISUALIZATION

Close your eyes and imagine yourself walking through the winding cobblestone streets of Oia, Santorini. The stones are warm beneath your feet, uneven but grounding, reminding you that you're standing in a place where thousands of years of history have already whispered abundance into the earth.

You pause, and in front of you is a doorway. Sunlight pours through it like a golden invitation, and on the other side, the Aegean Sea stretches endlessly in every direction. The water is the kind of blue you didn't know existed, brilliant, alive, sparkling with possibility. A table waits for you, perfectly prepared, as if it were always meant to be yours. Notice the crisp white linens, the gleam of the glassware, the way the chair pulls out effortlessly, as though the universe itself is saying: Sit, this was prepared for you.

You sink into the chair. Feel the breeze brush across your skin, carrying hints of sea salt from the Aegean. The sun warms your face, soft but steady, as if reminding you that abundance is always shining upon you. When the waiter sets down your plate, take in the vibrant colors, the deep red of tomatoes, the golden olive oil glistening, the fragrant herbs rising to meet your senses. With every bite, you're not just eating food. You're savoring abundance in its simplest form.

You're savoring evidence that life rises up to meet you when you allow yourself to receive.

Now, shift the scene. You're stepping into the helicopter. Slide the headset on and hear the muffled hum of anticipation. The blades begin to whirl above you, faster and faster, creating a rush of wind that whips your hair around your face. Your stomach flutters as the helicopter lifts, that exhilarating mix of nerves and excitement that always comes with rising higher.

Look out the window. Watch as the cliffs of Amorgos shrink below you, the whitewashed houses dotting the island like tiny specks of possibility. The old identity, the one who played small, who believed she had to be less than, grows smaller and smaller, too. You are leaving her behind with every upward pull.

Breathe deeply into this moment. Feel the vibration of the helicopter in your body, reminding you that movement and momentum are on your side. Feel the sun flooding the cabin, lighting you up from the inside out. With each inhale, know this truth. I am wealth. I am expansion. I am the woman who always says yes to her soul.

Stay here for a few breaths, letting your body memorize the feeling of rising, of expansion, of claiming the seat that was always meant for you. When you're ready, open your eyes and step into your day, carrying this energy with you.

Abundant B Mantra

> I release the old me who played small. Playing small is no longer my story. Big, bold, abundant living is who I am.

This isn't just my story. I've watched women I've worked with release the same beliefs, the ones that whisper you have to stay small, hide your brilliance, or be "less than" in order to be safe. When they stopped waiting for the proof and started being wealth, everything changed.

Autumn had to release the belief that making more money would cost her everything, her energy, her joy, even herself. That story kept her hiding from new opportunities, avoiding clients, and staying smaller than she wanted. But when she reframed wealth as something expansive, including self-care, joy, and brave investments in herself, she stopped being "less than." She became lighter, more creative, and more magnetic. Opportunities flowed toward her because she had stepped into a new way of being.

Lily's transformation came when she released the belief that survival was all she could expect. Month after month, she struggled just to get by, shrinking her vision to match her circumstances. But when she stopped waiting for proof and decided to embody the woman who already believed wealth was possible, she broke free. She tripled her income twice, yes, but even more importantly, she stopped being "less than" her potential. She began living as if her success was inevitable, and it became so. She expected success, and the universe met her where she was.

Hailey carried a deeply ingrained story that she wasn't allowed to out-earn her mom. That invisible ceiling kept her small, stuck, and playing safe for years. But when she released that belief, everything changed. She gave herself permission to rise, to claim more, and to stop hiding behind false limits. She stepped into passion again, opened her heart to receiving, and allowed herself to create a life and business far beyond what she once thought possible.

These women didn't just grow their income. They released the beliefs that kept them small, hidden, or less than who they truly are. They stepped into wealth as an identity. And like me in

Greece, they embodied the truth that playing small is no longer the story.

Guess what, Abundant B? Wealth isn't out there waiting for you to finally "earn it." Wealth is you. It's the identity you choose every morning when your feet hit the floor. It's the way you carry yourself before the results show up. It's the boldness in your choices, the joy in your presence, and the power in the way you say yes to your own life.

The moment you decide to stop shrinking and start shining, the universe moves. Doors open. Opportunities appear. Money doesn't just trickle in, it flows in like a river.

Let's make it official. Say it with me. I am done with playing small. I am done with hiding. I am done with believing I have to be less than. I am wealth. I am expansion. I am the woman who always rises.

Take a deep breath. Feel it in your body. Own it. Because the truth is, you don't need permission to step into your next level. You get to declare it. You get to live it. You get to play big, right now.

This is the moment you stop waiting for wealth to arrive and start being the Abundant B you already are.

And here's the best part, sweet Abundant B, this journey doesn't stop here. You've stepped into your new identity, and now it's time to turn the dial even higher. In the next chapter, we'll dive into the practices that keep you anchored in abundance, so it flows on repeat. And we're starting with one of the most magnetic forces in manifestation: gratitude.

Remember, being wealthy isn't a one-time decision… It's a way of living. And once you step into it, there's no going back.

Wealth isn't something you chase. It's something you embody and attract.

chapter ten

GRATITUDE: THE MULTIPLIER OF MONEY AND MIRACLES

Gratitude is the gateway to abundance. But let's be honest, Abundant B, sometimes gratitude feels hard to access. When you're in a negative mindset, when bills are piling up, or when life feels heavy, the last thing your brain wants to do is make a list of things to be thankful for. I know it's hard. I hear this from clients all the time.

The truth is, you don't have to reach for the "big wins" to find gratitude. You can dial it all the way back down to your basic needs. Every month, I contribute to two charities that support children who don't even have access to running water. Think about that for a moment. We walk to the faucet, and clean water flows instantly. Something so simple, so ordinary, is actually extraordinary when you pause to notice it.

Gratitude doesn't have to start with six-figure launches or dream vacations. It can begin with breath in your lungs, water in your glass, a roof over your head, or your loved ones being safe.

And the moment you shift into gratitude, no matter how small, your energy changes. That's when abundance begins to flow.

The most powerful gratitude is often the simplest. The inhale and exhale that prove you're alive. The sun that rose this morning without you having to lift a finger. The food on your table. The electricity that lights your home. The friend who texted to check on you.

Here's what I've seen over and over: when you start small, gratitude snowballs. You begin with "I'm grateful for my coffee this morning." The next thought might be, "I'm grateful I have the money to buy it." Then, "I'm grateful for the barista who made it," and "I'm grateful I get to start my workday doing something I love." One spark of gratitude ignites another, and soon your whole perspective shifts.

Gratitude isn't just a mindset trick; it's an energetic shift. When you focus on what's working, what you love, and what's already here, your brain releases feel-good chemicals like dopamine and serotonin. Your nervous system begins to calm. Suddenly, you're no longer spiraling in stress about what you lack. You're anchored in the truth that you are supported right now.

And here's why this matters for you as a business owner. Dopamine and serotonin aren't just "happy chemicals." They directly influence your ability to think clearly, make bold decisions, and stay creative under pressure. When dopamine is flowing, your brain is more motivated to take inspired action and follow through. When serotonin levels rise, you feel calmer, more confident, and more capable of handling challenges. Together, they shift you out of survival mode and into a state where ideas can flow, solutions can appear, and opportunities feel possible. In other words, gratitude doesn't just help you feel good. It helps you lead better, create better, and manifest better.

Science confirms what spiritual teachers have always said —What you appreciate, appreciates you. In fact, researchers at the University of California, Davis found that people who kept a daily gratitude journal experienced 25% higher levels of happiness, better sleep, and lower stress hormones compared to those who focused on problems. And the Heart Math Institute discovered that practicing gratitude for just five minutes creates measurable changes in your heart rhythms, shifting the body into coherence. In that state, your nervous system calms, stress melts away, and you literally become more magnetic.

Gratitude doesn't just feel good. It makes you a magnet for abundance. When you send out the signal that says, "I am thankful, I see the abundance already around me," you attract more of it. Clients. Opportunities. Ideas. Money. Relationships. Gratitude multiplies everything it touches. And the more magnetic you become, the faster manifestations flow in, often in ways you couldn't have planned or forced if you tried. That's the magic of gratitude.

Gratitude is not just a concept. It's a practice. And like any practice, the more you do it, the stronger it becomes. It's not about writing a perfect journal entry every morning or keeping an elaborate list of thank-yous taped to your wall. It's about training your brain and body to notice abundance everywhere.

You can start small. Write down three things you're grateful for before bed. Go on a "gratitude walk" and speak out loud the things you notice, the sparkle of the trees, the kiss of fresh air, the quiet space to think, the little bird or critter that crosses your path like a divine wink. Take a deep breath in the middle of a busy day and thank your body for carrying you. These small acts rewire your brain to search for what's good instead of fixating on what's wrong.

This is also why I love gratitude prompts. A good prompt doesn't just ask what you're thankful for. It drops you right into the energy of awareness and flips the switch from autopilot to pure magic. One day, the prompt might guide you to notice what you're receiving. Another day, it might ask what you're proud of. Over time, those questions shape your thoughts. Instead of looking for lack, you begin scanning your life for proof of abundance. And as soon as you see it, you start to feel it.

Gratitude doesn't erase challenges. It doesn't mean you pretend everything is perfect. It means that even in the middle of uncertainty, you choose to notice what's here. It's like building an inner safety net of gratitude that catches you when things feel shaky, and it lifts you higher when things feel heavy. It's a daily reset button for your energy.

And here's the fun part: your journal becomes more than a record. It becomes a magnet. By writing down your gratitude, you're signaling to your subconscious that this is what matters, what we notice, and what we multiply. What you track grows substantially. Gratitude journaling is your personal highlight reel, your daily celebration, and your secret manifestation power all in one.

If you love the idea of prompts to guide your gratitude practice, you're going to love what's coming next. In the following section of this book, I'll be sharing 70 energy prompts and mantras you can use for the next 70 days to stay in the energy of abundance. With each one, I'll also share a takeaway or two from one of my clients, along with space for you to write your own reflections. Think of it as a guided practice, a personal love note to your future self, a daily conversation with yourself that will expand your capacity to notice and receive.

And here's where we take it even deeper. Gratitude isn't only about noticing what's here; it's also about giving thanks for what's coming. It's called quantum gratitude. You can thank the clients who haven't arrived yet, the opportunities that are already making their way to you, and the money that is lining up to flow into your account. This is gratitude in advance. A pre-order of miracles. This isn't fantasy, it's alignment. It's training your mind and energy to recognize the future as already available.

And yes, science backs this up. A study conducted by the University of Zürich and Washington University followed more than 300 adults over two weeks. On days when participants felt their futures were wide open with opportunities, they also reported significantly higher levels of gratitude. Even more fascinating? Those effects carried over into the next day, proof that gratitude and a positive sense of the future fuel one another.

Another study by the University of São Paulo in Brazil combined 64 clinical trials and found that gratitude practices, such as journaling, are consistently linked to higher optimism, stronger emotional well-being, and lower stress. Which means that when you keep a gratitude journal, especially one that includes things you're thankful for before they arrive, you're not just writing nice words on a page. You are literally scripting your future, rewiring your brain, and magnetizing your energy with the abundance that's already on its way.

Try this simple practice tonight and watch what shifts. Before bed, write down three things you're grateful for right now and one thing you're grateful for in advance. Thank it as if it's already here. This single practice can shift your entire state and open the door for abundance to meet you.

You can also weave gratitude into your mornings and evenings so it becomes the rhythm of your day.

MORNING GRATITUDE RITUAL

Before you even pick up your phone, place your hand on your heart and name three things you're grateful for. They don't have to be big: the softness of your pillow, the warmth of your coffee, the fact that you get another day to create. Let yourself feel that gratitude before your feet hit the floor. This sets your nervous system into calm, creative energy instead of rushing into stress.

EVENING GRATITUDE RITUAL

Right before bed, reflect on your day. Ask yourself, "What went well today?" and "What am I grateful to release?" Write down at least three things. The first anchors you in appreciation, the second clears your energy so you don't carry stress into sleep. You'll drift off lighter and wake up more open to receive.

Abundant B Prompt

What blessings am I overlooking right now?

This single question shifts your lens from lack to abundance. It reminds you that no matter what is happening, you are already supported in more ways than you realize.

For the audio version of the following visualization, please visit my book portal:

GRATITUDE VISUALIZATION

Close your eyes and take a slow, steady breath. Place your hand on your heart and imagine a soft golden light glowing there, like a warm flame. With every inhale, that light grows brighter, warmer, and steadier. With every exhale, the light expands, filling your chest with ease. Soon it begins to flow beyond your heart, into your arms, your legs, your entire body, until you are glowing from the inside out.

Now bring to mind one thing you are grateful for right now. It can be simple: the roof over your head, the sound of laughter, the fact that you have this moment to breathe. See it clearly. Let your mind picture it. Feel it in your body. Notice how the golden light pulses stronger as you sit in thankfulness for this gift.

Next, bring to mind one thing you are grateful for in advance. Something you deeply desire, something you know is already on its way. Imagine it as if it has already arrived: the joy of the email confirming the new client, the peace of seeing your bank account grow, the excitement of a long-held dream finally being realized. Let yourself feel it in every cell, as though it is happening now. Whisper a quiet thank you, as though it's already yours.

Now imagine the golden light expanding outward, beyond your body, beyond the room you are in, sending ripples of gratitude into the world. See that energy moving like waves, circling back to you multiplied. Gratitude out, abundance in. Gratitude out, abundance in. Over and over again, a beautiful rhythm of giving and receiving.

Rest here for a few more breaths, soaking in the truth that you are supported, guided, and deeply provided for. Gratitude is not just something you practice. It is who you are.

When you're ready, open your eyes and carry that golden light with you into the rest of your day.

Abundant B Mantra

> Gratitude is my superpower. The more I notice it, the more abundance flows to me.

There was a season in my own journey where gratitude felt like the only thing I could hold onto. When I made the decision to release my CFO retainers and step fully into coaching, I suddenly found myself without the steady income I had relied on for years. Month by month, I had to dip into my savings to keep things afloat. And I'll be honest, at first it scared me. It felt like failure, like everything I had built was slipping through my fingers.

But one day, in the middle of that fear, I had a revelation. Instead of spiraling over the money leaving my account, I chose to be grateful that it was there in the first place. My savings weren't evidence of failure; it was evidence of past success. It was proof that I had built a strong foundation, and that foundation was now giving me the gift of space and time to grow into my next season. A season that truly invigorates my soul.

The moment I shifted into gratitude, the panic loosened its grip. I began to see my savings not as something I was losing, but as something that was supporting me. That gratitude softened my energy and gave me the courage to keep going. And not long after, new opportunities began to flow in, opportunities that wouldn't have had space to arrive if I had stayed clinging to the old.

Autumn also experienced this shift firsthand. When she first came into my world, she thought gratitude meant being thankful only when money was flowing in. If income was up, she felt grateful. If income was down, she struggled. What she didn't realize was that her focus on only financial gratitude kept her blind to the river of abundance already surrounding her.

As she began to practice gratitude more intentionally, something clicked. She started noticing abundance in every corner of her life, the beauty in a quiet walk, the ease in her daily routines, even the opportunities her partner was creating in his own career. That last part was a big breakthrough. Autumn realized she had been unconsciously blocking her partner's abundance. Somewhere deep down, she had attached her worth to being the primary provider, and it made her tense whenever he succeeded.

The moment she shifted into gratitude for his wins, everything in her relaxed. "It was like my whole body softened," she told me. "The resistance I didn't even know I was carrying just lifted." From that place of gratitude, happiness became her default setting. Ideas began flowing. Opportunities opened up. She no longer felt she had to control or force everything.

That's the power of gratitude. It doesn't just change your perspective, it also changes the energy you radiate. And when your energy changes, your reality follows.

Gratitude is the spark that ignites abundance into a flame.

Hailey discovered that gratitude could become a daily practice woven right into her routine. Inside our private Money Mindset and Manifestation Accelerator group, I send out daily prompts designed to shift mindset and energy, and she began using them as her "gratitude activators." She told me that more than once, a manifestation would arrive while she was literally in the middle of answering a prompt. It was as if the act of noticing what she was grateful for in real time sent out a signal to the universe that brought her desires straight to her door.

One of the biggest shifts for Hailey came on vacation. In the past, she believed that abundance and business success only happened when she was hustling, working, or glued to her laptop. Vacation meant falling behind, losing momentum, or missing opportunities. But through the practice of gratitude, she began to experience something new. She stayed present, practiced thankfulness, and let herself actually receive the rest and joy of being away. And to her surprise, abundance still flowed in. She made money on vacation, something she had never thought possible.

What she loved most was the group energy of our Accelerator. "It multiplies it by 10,000," she said. Gratitude in community isn't just one person celebrating; it's an energetic amplifier. Each woman's gratitude fuels the next, creating a current so strong you can't help but be carried forward.

Gratitude multiplies everything it touches.

Lily described gratitude as the practice that reconnected her to what she called the "universal abundance current." She realized that abundance wasn't something she had to chase; it was always available, constantly flowing, and gratitude was the way to plug back in.

On the days when business felt heavy or her confidence wavered, it was the group prompts that kept her grounded. They became daily reminders to notice what was working and to stay connected to the flow, even when her mind wanted to spiral.

The more she leaned into gratitude, the more her energy shifted. Her confidence returned. Invitations to speak at summits, podcast interviews, and new clients started coming in almost effortlessly. Gratitude had moved her from searching for opportunities to receiving them.

Gratitude is the bridge between who you are today and the abundance you're calling in tomorrow.

Gratitude isn't just something you do; it's who you are becoming. It's the frequency that turns ordinary moments into miracles and simple thank-yous into rivers of overflow. The more you live it, the more magnetic you become. The more you embody it, the more abundance rushes to meet you. Gratitude is the foundation, the activator, the spark. And when you anchor into it, Abundant B, you don't just attract more, you become the woman who can hold it all.

Now it's time to take everything you've learned and put it into daily practice. In the next section of this book, I'm giving you a guided 70-Day Money Manifestation Activation. Think of it as a personal activation guide, part challenge, part journal, part conversation with your future self. Every page will hold a new prompt and mantra, drawn from the same practices that have transformed my clients inside the Money Mindset and Manifestation Accelerator. You'll see anonymous examples from their journeys, and you'll have space to reflect on your own.

This isn't theory anymore, it's embodiment. Seventy days of rewiring your thoughts, aligning your energy, and stepping fully into the Abundant B you were born to be. Welcome to Part Four, Abundant B!

part four

MONEY MANIFESTATION ACTIVATION—70 DAYS OF ABUNDANCE

Alright, Abundant B, this is where we unleash your attraction energy.

Remember the Emotional Scale we discussed in Chapter 4? To maximize manifestation, your goal is to stay at the top of the scale in positive energy 51% of the time. Each one of the following 70 days of Energy Prompts is designed to align your energy with the positive emotions on the Scale.

These prompts were first created inside my Money Mindset and Manifestation Accelerator. Every weekday, I pop into our group and drop a short, powerful message paired with a mantra. Sometimes it's a journal prompt. Sometimes it's an activity or a bold declaration to repeat, which I call activations.

And let me tell you, the women really love them. These quick little prompts and activations have become their secret weapon. They've shifted moods, rewired old patterns, and opened doors to more money, more opportunities, and more ease. Now it's your turn.

Here's how this works:

- At the top of each page, you'll see a prompt and a mantra or an activation. Some prompts will ask you to reflect and journal, others will invite you to take a small or fun action, or maybe repeat a powerful statement.
- Challenge yourself to commit to all 70 days. Each one takes just a few minutes, but it will completely change how you start your mornings—and how money flows into your life.
- Alongside these prompts, listen to your Financial Abundance Audio from Chapter 7 every single day. The repetition is key. The audio reprograms your subconscious while the prompts shift your daily energy. Together, they're a powerhouse practice.
- Below are some prompts. You'll find quotes from clients for your "inspiration." Let their words inspire you and remind you what's possible.
- Then, use the blank lines provided to capture your own reflections, breakthroughs, or inspired ideas.

And if you want to go all in, I've got a printable workbook waiting for you inside the book portal with space to journal every day and to keep your experiences in one place.

Abundance loves consistency. The more you show up for this practice, the more the universe shows up for you. Day after day, you're raising your vibration, rewiring your beliefs, and stepping into the frequency where miracles happen.

And please don't keep it to yourself. I want to celebrate with you. Find me on social media or reach out through my website. Share your stories, your wins, your "oh my gosh this worked!" moments. Nothing inspires me more than seeing women stepping into their abundance and owning it.

So grab your favorite pen, claim these next 70 days as yours, and start looking for miracles.

Are you ready? Whee… here we go!

DAY 1–THE ENERGY OF LOVE

Prompt:

What do you love about yourself? Write down at least three things.

Mantra for the Day:

The more I love myself, the more abundance flows to me.

Inspiration:

When I first gave this prompt inside my Money Mindset & Manifestation Accelerator, many women found it surprisingly difficult. But abundance begins with receiving your own worth.

One client shared this beautiful reflection:

"I love my creative big picture energy. I am always trying my best. I never give up. I learn from my mistakes. I am grateful my body can heal from physical and emotional trauma. I am grateful I get to help so many women release weight, and diet narratives, and diet trauma without counting or tracking anything."

Now it's your turn. What do you love about yourself today?

____

____

____

____

____

____

Don't forget: Listen to your Financial Abundance Audio today.

DAY 2—THE ENERGY OF ABUNDANCE

Prompt:

What abundance do you notice today? Make note of all the abundant things you see around you. It could be money or anything at all.

Mantra for the Day:

I live in a world overflowing with abundance, and it's all around me.

Inspiration:

Clients shared:

"I'm grateful for the abundance of time today to work on projects without distractions, the love my dog gives me, and the support of friends during a challenging week."

"I have an abundance of helicopters (from trees)!!! Millions! And they keep falling!!! Soon I'll have an abundance of maple sprouts!"

Now it's your turn. What abundance are you noticing today?

____

____

____

____

____

____

Don't forget: Listen to your Financial Abundance Audio today.

DAY 3—THE ENERGY OF WORTHINESS

Activation:

Say this out loud three times, slowly and with conviction, like Dorothy clicking her heels together in The Wizard of Oz:

"I am worthy of receiving more abundance than I have ever received in my entire life."

Stand tall, shoulders back. Place a hand on your heart. Breathe it in between each repetition and notice the shift in your body, warmth in your chest, steadier breath, a little more lift in your posture. Let the words land and expand. Then make it yours by writing the sentence repeatedly until it feels true in your bones.

Where can you honor your worthiness more boldly today?

____

____

____

____

____

____

____

____

____

Don't forget: Listen to your Financial Abundance Audio today.

DAY 4–THE ENERGY OF EMPOWERMENT

Prompt:

Imagine your next-level self. What does she know? What does she believe? How does she feel?

Mantra for the Day:

I already hold the wisdom, beliefs, and power of my next-level self.

Inspiration:

Clients shared:

"*My next-level self knows that everyone wants to work with me. She believes that she is worthy of receiving abundance. She feels fulfilled.*"

"*She knows she is consistently showing up and taking action towards her dreams. She is worthy of abundance. She believes all of her investments in herself will come back to her tenfold.*"

Now it's your turn. What does your next-level self know, believe, and feel?

____

____

____

____

____

Don't forget: Listen to your Financial Abundance Audio today.

DAY 5–THE ENERGY OF JOY

Activation:

Do one thing for fun today: sing, dance, laugh, or play!

Joy is the best abundance magnet. Think of it like turning up the dial on your vibration. The more joy you feel, the more magnetic you become to everything you desire.

Play Space:

Use the space below to jot down what you did for fun, how it felt, or any little moments of joy that surprised you today.

____

____

____

____

____

____

____

____

____

____

____

Don't forget: Listen to your Financial Abundance Audio today.

DAY 6—THE ENERGY OF POSITIVE EXPECTATIONS

Prompt:

Reflect on a time you felt financially abundant—big or small—and celebrate that memory!

Mantra for the Day:

> *The more I celebrate my abundance, the more abundance celebrates me.*

Inspiration:

Here's what two clients shared when they tried this prompt:

"My memory of financial abundance is from 2023 when I went from literally $20 in my bank account to my first $20k month within 6 months."

"I felt financially abundant right before my divorce when my business took off, and I could afford a beach vacation for my family and me with all my own earnings!"

Now it's your turn. What memory of financial abundance will you celebrate today?

____

____

____

____

____

____

Don't forget: Listen to your Financial Abundance Audio today.

DAY 7–THE ENERGY OF GRATITUDE

Activation:

Send a personal thank-you note or message to someone who has impacted your life. As you do, notice how it makes you feel because giving always opens the door to receiving.

Bonus Challenge (if you are up to it):

See how many thank-you notes you can send today.

Reflection Space:

Use the space below to jot down who you reached out to, how it felt to send gratitude, and anything that shifted for you as a result.

____

____

____

____

____

____

____

____

Don't forget: Listen to your Financial Abundance Audio today.

DAY 8–THE ENERGY OF ENTHUSIASM

Prompt:

Celebrate a win, big or small! Remember, celebrating what you already have brings in more abundance.

Mantra for the Day:

> *The more I celebrate, the more the universe gives me to celebrate.*

Inspiration:

Clients celebrated:

"A corporate client paying on time and receiving full payment for the work."

"Three clients in one week!"

"A breakthrough in creativity I know will bring financial success."

"A better relationship with myself through challenges."

Now it's your turn. What win can you celebrate today?

____

____

____

____

____

____

____

Don't forget: Listen to your Financial Abundance Audio today.

DAY 9–THE ENERGY OF MONEY

Activation:

Write a note to money. Thank it, love it, and invite more of it to come into your life. Think of it like writing a love letter to your most loyal partner, the one who always shows up for you.

Inspiration:

Here's an example one client wrote when she tried this activation:

"Dear Money,

Thank you for always supporting me, even when I didn't see you there. I love the freedom and opportunities you bring into my life. I welcome more of you to flow to me with ease, and I promise to treat you with respect and gratitude. Love always."

Now it's your turn. What would you like to say to money today?

____

____

____

____

____

____

____

____

Don't forget: Listen to your Financial Abundance Audio today.

DAY 10–THE ENERGY OF LOVE

Prompt:

What do you love in your life, your work, and your environment today?

Mantra for the Day:

The more I love my life, the more my life loves me back.

Inspiration:

Clients shared:

"I'm about to publish my 7th article on a topic I love."

"I love the ocean, even in the rain—it's still gorgeous and majestic."

"My fresh, clean bedsheets."

"This group of amazing women has become my daily pocket of inspiration."

"Tapping is transforming so much for me—physically and mentally."

Now it's your turn. What are the things you love most today?

____

____

____

____

____

____

Don't forget: Listen to your Financial Abundance Audio today.

DAY 11–THE ENERGY OF OPTIMISM

Prompt:

Imagine the perfect client finding you today. How do they feel? How do you feel? How excited are both of you to work together?

Mantra for the Day:

> *My dream clients find me with ease, and we are thrilled to work together.*

Inspiration:

One client shared:

"The perfect client is finding me today… after reading my post, they feel seen. I feel certain I can help them, and we are so freaking excited to work together that we start immediately. I'm so excited to support her. I cleared space in my calendar to set up our initial call, and she knows this is right this time." (Within two minutes of answering this prompt, she got a message from a new client ready to work with her).

Now it's your turn. Imagine your perfect client finding you today. How do they feel? How do you feel?

____

____

____

____

____

Don't forget: Listen to your Financial Abundance Audio today.

DAY 12—THE ENERGY OF EMPOWERMENT

Activation:

Stand tall, shoulders back, and declare out loud:

"I am worthy of overflow."

Don't just say it. Yell it, scream it, embody it. Feel the shift in your posture, in your breath, in your presence. When you imagine and declare your worth, you open yourself up to receive.

The universe responds to the energy you carry, and when you declare your worthiness, you magnetize more than enough into your life. Overflow isn't just for someone else—it's for you, too.

Now write about how it feels to embody worthiness. What shifts when you imagine yourself living from a place of overflow?

____

____

____

____

____

____

____

____

____

____

Don't forget: Listen to your Financial Abundance Audio today.

DAY 13–THE ENERGY OF FREEDOM

Prompt:

Where can you create space in your life or in your business to allow something new to come in?

Mantra for the Day:

The more space I create, the more abundance flows in.

We can't call in the new while clinging to the old. Sometimes abundance begins with clearing out, whether it's a cluttered closet, a jam-packed calendar, or habits that no longer serve you.

Inspiration:

Clients shared:

"I can spend less time tinkering with landing pages, website, pricing, and offers, and more time on high-impact work like reach-outs and nurturing."

"I'm committing to clearing my personal closet today, letting go of old stuff, and even cleaning out my wallet to make space for new."

Now it's your turn. Where will you create space today?

____

____

____

____

Don't forget: Listen to your Financial Abundance Audio today.

DAY 14–THE ENERGY OF RECEIVING

Activation:

Say yes to something small today: help, an opportunity, or even a compliment. Practice receiving with openness and gratitude.

Receiving can feel vulnerable, but it is one of the most powerful ways to expand abundance. Every time you say "yes" with an open heart, you reinforce the belief that you are supported and worthy. Start small and watch how your energy shifts.

Now, write about what you received today and how it felt to allow it in. Did it feel easy? Uncomfortable? Joyful?

Don't forget: Listen to your Financial Abundance Audio today.

DAY 15—THE ENERGY OF HOPEFULNESS

Prompt:

If it were easy, how would you show up in your business and life?

Mantra for the Day:

When I choose ease, abundance flows effortlessly to me.

Inspiration:

Clients shared:

"If it were easy, I'd ask people if they want to work with me without overthinking or trying to convince them."

"If it is easy, my clients will be lining up to work with me, and I'd have a waitlist!!"

"If it were easy, I could relax into it and enjoy the ride, exactly what I'm teaching my clients."

Now it's your turn. What would shift if you allowed it to be easy?

____

____

____

____

____

____

Don't forget: Listen to your Financial Abundance Audio today.

DAY 16—THE ENERGY OF APPRECIATION

Prompt:

Make a list of the things you get to do today. Shifting from "I have to" into "I get to" instantly changes your energy and opens the door for more joy and abundance.

Mantra for the Day:

I get to live, create, and receive with joy.

Inspiration:

One client shared how her day transformed when she shifted into "I get to":

"Today I get to coach a private client, connect with someone new, create a free gift with ease, enjoy a delicious lunch already waiting for me, send a fun bonus email, and finish the day supporting a client preparing for her big event. That is a lot of fun and creative energy I GET to be in and share!"

Now it's your turn. What do you get to do today?

____

____

____

____

____

____

Don't forget: Listen to your Financial Abundance Audio today.

DAY 17—THE ENERGY OF SURRENDER

Prompt:

How are you going to let go of the "how" and practice surrender today?

Mantra for the Day:

I release the how and trust the flow.

Inspiration:

One client shared:

"I am surrendering my in-person workshop and book launch dinner. I'm surrendering the how and am going to meditate on what to do."

Now it's your turn. Where can you let go and practice surrender today?

____

____

____

____

____

____

____

Don't forget: Listen to your Financial Abundance Audio today.

DAY 18–THE ENERGY OF GRATITUDE

Prompt:

List three unexpected blessings that came to you this year.

Mantra for the Day:

Unexpected blessings flow to me with ease.

Inspiration:

Clients shared blessings like:

"My world has expanded, and I've connected with inspiring peers."

"Being self-employed means I'm home more for my teenager, and our relationship is stronger."

"Training as a coach gave me the superpower of self-coaching and shifting my own mindsets."

Now it's your turn. What unexpected blessings are you celebrating?

____

____

____

____

____

____

____

Don't forget: Listen to your Financial Abundance Audio today.

DAY 19–THE ENERGY OF SELF-APPRECIATION

Prompt:

Finish the sentence: *"I am proud of myself for…"*

Mantra for the Day:

I honor how far I've come and all that I've created.

Inspiration:

Clients shared:

"I am proud of myself for writing a book and running a business all by myself!"

"I am proud of not giving up, even when I wanted to throw in the towel."

"I keep trusting that the world needs my work, and that I will be repaid with abundance and freedom."

Now it's your turn. What are you proud of yourself for?

____

____

____

____

____

____

____

Don't forget: Listen to your Financial Abundance Audio today.

DAY 20–THE ENERGY OF EMPOWERMENT

Prompt:

What powerful and positive statement can you make to finish this sentence, *"I deserve…"*

Mantra for the Day:

I am deserving of all the joy, wealth, and freedom I desire.

Inspiration:

Clients shared:

"I deserve happiness, peace, comfort, and abundance."
"I deserve to take time off for rest and self-care."
"I deserve aligned, high-paying clients who value me."
"I deserve a beautiful home, family travel, and financial freedom."
Now it's your turn. What do you deserve?

____

____

____

____

____

____

____

Don't forget: Listen to your Financial Abundance Audio today.

DAY 21–THE ENERGY OF EXPANSION

Prompt:

I am ready for more because…

Mantra for the Day:

I am ready for more abundance, and more is ready for me.

Inspiration:

Clients shared:

"I am ready for more because I am powerful beyond measure, and my business is built to hold abundance."

"I am ready for more because I see how much women need this transformation, and I want to make a difference in their lives."

"I am ready for more because I deserve to provide for my family with ease and love."

Now it's your turn. Why are you ready for more?

____

____

____

____

____

____

____

***Don't forget: Listen** to your Financial Abundance Audio today.*

DAY 22–THE ENERGY OF POSITIVE EXPECTATION

Prompt:

Align your energy with what you are calling in. What's one loving action or intention you're setting today to welcome in more abundance, ease, joy, or support from the Universe?

Mantra for the Day:

> *I align my energy with abundance, and abundance aligns with me.*

Inspiration:

Clients shared:

"I'm calling in being open and really listening to my intuition."

"My aligned action is reaching out to potential clients to support them on their journey."

Now it's your turn. What aligned action or intention will you set today?

____

____

____

____

____

____

____

Don't forget: Listen to your Financial Abundance Audio today.

DAY 23—THE ENERGY OF RECEIVING

Prompt:

Imagine receiving $10,000 today, no strings attached. What's the first thing you'd do? How would it feel in your body?

Mantra for the Day:

I joyfully receive unexpected money with ease.

Inspiration:

Clients shared:

"My body feels elated and at ease. I'd celebrate and fully relax on vacation with my family."

"I'd feel grateful and peaceful, pay expenses, save some, and enjoy the summer with calm and joy."

Now it's your turn. Imagine receiving $10K today. How does it feel?

____

____

____

____

____

____

____

Don't forget: Listen to your Financial Abundance Audio today.

DAY 24–THE ENERGY OF FREEDOM

Activation:

Look at your calendar. What can you clear, cancel, or delegate to create more space for abundance to flow in over the next few days? Sometimes it's not about doing more. It's about doing less, but with intention.

Inspiration:

Clients shared:

"I released clutter in my office, and it felt spacious and fresh."

"I let go of the fear of not working enough, and a potential client reached out right after."

Now it's your turn. What can you release to create space for magic to come in?

____

____

____

____

____

____

____

____

Don't forget: Listen to your Financial Abundance Audio today.

DAY 25—THE ENERGY OF BELIEF

Prompt:

Write down one money belief that is holding you back. Cross it out and replace it with an empowering one.

Mantra for the Day:

I choose beliefs that expand abundance in my life.

Inspiration:

Clients shared:

"Old belief: I can't generate money when I need it. New belief: I generate more than enough, and my bills are paid with ease."

"Old belief: It's hard to make consistent money. New belief: Money flows to me easily and joyfully."

"Old belief: I have to do more to receive more. New belief: The more I expect with certainty, the more money I receive!"

Now it's your turn. What belief will you rewrite today?

____

____

____

____

____

____

____

Don't forget: Listen to your Financial Abundance Audio today.

DAY 26–THE ENERGY OF POSITIVE EXPECTATION

Prompt:

Visualize your bank account, calendar, and energy overflowing with exactly what you desire. What do you see? How does it feel?

Mantra for the Day:

I see it, I feel it, I live it—overflow is mine.

Inspiration:

Clients shared:

"I see $20,000 flowing in monthly. My calendar is full of fun work, and I feel secure, joyous, and grateful."

"I see over $300,000 in my accounts, which makes me feel excited, free, and comfortable."

"I see £25,000 per month, working four days a week, traveling with my family, and buying our dream home."

Now it's your turn. Visualize it, what do you see and feel?

Don't forget: Listen to your Financial Abundance Audio today.

DAY 27—THE ENERGY OF HOPEFULNESS

Activation:

Take five deep breaths, and with each one, imagine yourself receiving exactly what you desire with ease.

Inspiration:

Clients shared desires like:

"Attracting 12 founding members into our program."
"Effortlessly creating our digital platform."
"Confidence to deliver a transformational experience."

Now it's your turn. Breathe in your desires. What are you calling in?

____

____

____

____

____

____

____

____

____

____

Don't forget: Listen to your Financial Abundance Audio today.

DAY 28—THE ENERGY OF PASSION

Prompt:

What makes you magnetic? Own it, say it, and celebrate it.

Mantra for the Day:

My unique energy makes me magnetic to all that I desire.

Inspiration:

Clients shared:

"My openness and compassion."

"My approachable demeanor and ability to bring amazing women together."

"The way I make people feel seen, loved, and supported."

Now it's your turn. What makes you magnetic?

____

____

____

____

____

____

____

Don't forget: Listen to your Financial Abundance Audio today.

DAY 29—THE ENERGY OF TRUST

Activation:

Take a deep breath, then say this out loud:
"Everything I desire is already on its way."
Then really feel it in your body and nervous system.

Inspiration:

Clients shared:

"I've had my eye on a new home. It feels so real, I can already feel myself living there."

"I desire a paid speaking gig in the next 6 weeks, and I can already feel it happening."

Now it's your turn. Say it, feel it, and believe it.

____

____

____

____

____

____

____

____

Don't forget: Listen to your Financial Abundance Audio today.

DAY 30–THE ENERGY OF LOVE

Activation:

What you give, you receive. Go through your day being your most generous self, whether it's sharing kindness, celebrating others, or giving love freely. Notice how it feels.

Inspiration:

Clients shared:

"Celebrating my husband receiving a surprise consulting work."
"Appreciating my partner for doing the dishes."
"Telling my dad how amazing he is."
Now it's your turn. How will you embody generosity today?

____

____

____

____

____

____

____

____

Don't forget: Listen to your Financial Abundance Audio today.

DAY 31—THE ENERGY OF HOPEFULNESS

Prompt:

What is one thing you can do to shift your energy today?

Mantra for the Day:

> *Every small shift lifts my energy and aligns me with abundance.*

Inspiration:

Clients shared:

"I'm going to lift my spirit by walking my dogs."

"I shifted my energy with tapping when I felt frustrated."

"I let myself relax with a silly show after a tough day—and it worked."

Now it's your turn. What will shift your energy today?

____

____

____

____

____

____

____

Don't forget: Listen to your Financial Abundance Audio today.

DAY 32—THE ENERGY OF APPRECIATION

Prompt:

List five things that remind you that abundance is all around you.

Mantra for the Day:

> *Appreciation opens the door for even more abundance to flow.*

Inspiration:

Clients shared:

"My home, pictures of my kids at camp, playing tennis outdoors, the wind in the trees, and happy dogs."

"My beautiful home, the trees and hills in my backyard, fun with my family, creating a unit for my dad, and the unconditional love of my puppies."

"24 years of marriage, vibrant green grass, seeing friends at the gym, freedom to work out with my daughter, and collaborating on a new program."

Now it's your turn. What five things remind you that abundance surrounds you today?

____

____

____

____

____

Don't forget: Listen to your Financial Abundance Audio today.

DAY 33–THE ENERGY OF BELIEF

Activation:

Write this, then say it out loud:
"I claim (monthly $ goal). I am ready. I am worthy. It is done."

Inspiration:

Clients shared:
"I claim $20,000 a month! I am ready. I am worthy. It is done!"
"I claim $15,000 a month. I am ready! I am worthy. It is done!"
Now it's your turn. Claim it, say it, and feel it in your body.

____

____

____

____

____

____

____

____

____

____

Don't forget: Listen to your Financial Abundance Audio today.

DAY 34—THE ENERGY OF POSITIVE EXPECTATION

Prompt:

Visualize money pouring in with ease. What does your life look like?

Mantra for the Day:

I expect money to flow easily into my life.

Inspiration:

Clients shared:

"I see multiple income streams flowing with ease. I'm realizing how valuable I am. I'm a money magnet!"

"I imagine debt-free living, investments, family trips, and a home filled with beauty and art."

Now it's your turn. What does your life look like with money flowing in easily?

____

____

____

____

____

____

____

Don't forget: Listen to your Financial Abundance Audio today.

DAY 35–THE ENERGY OF EMPOWERMENT

Prompt:

Reflect on your energetic growth. What feels different now?

Mantra for the Day:

I am empowered by how much I've grown.

Inspiration:

One Client shared:
"I feel better resourced to sit in uncertainty and stay grounded."
Now it's your turn. How has your energy shifted?

____

____

____

____

____

____

____

____

____

Don't forget: Listen to your Financial Abundance Audio today.

DAY 36–THE ENERGY OF GRATITUDE

Prompt:

List one (or several) things you once dreamed of that you now have. Give gratitude.

Mantra for the Day:

I love and appreciate the dreams I once had that are now my reality.

Inspiration:

Clients shared:

"Two healthy kids, my own business, a body I love, a passionate relationship, and a comfortable home."

"Two years ago, I dreamed of working for myself. Now I live it."

"Five years ago, I lived in a garage. Now I'm married and living in the most beautiful place."

Now it's your turn. What dreams have already come true for you?

____

____

____

____

____

____

Don't forget: Listen to your Financial Abundance Audio today.

DAY 37–THE ENERGY OF ABUNDANCE

Prompt:

What area of your life is already overflowing with abundance? Celebrate it.

Mantra for the Day:

I celebrate the abundance already overflowing in my life.

Inspiration:

Clients shared:

"My love life, my kids, my friendships, and my morning rituals."

"Looking at our net worth, I felt grateful knowing abundance is already here."

Now it's your turn. Where are you already overflowing?

____

____

____

____

____

____

____

____

Don't forget: Listen to your Financial Abundance Audio today.

DAY 38–THE ENERGY OF EXCITEMENT

Prompt:

Celebrate something unexpected that recently showed up.

Mantra for the Day:

> *Unexpected blessings excite me and remind me that abundance is everywhere.*

Inspiration:

Clients shared:

"A call from my best friend from elementary school."

"Being honored at a conference."

"Invited to lead a focus group and speak in a class."

Now it's your turn. What unexpected gift has shown up for you?

____

____

____

____

____

____

____

Don't forget: Listen to your Financial Abundance Audio today.

DAY 39–THE ENERGY OF LOVE

Activation:

Say kind, loving things to yourself all day. Share one nice thought.

Inspiration:

Clients shared:

"It's ok for my mind and body to rest. Vacation is important."

"I felt the urge to run again after two weeks, and I did!"

"Acknowledging God is in control of inflows and outflows felt energizing."

Now it's your turn. What kind and loving words will you say to yourself today?

____

____

____

____

____

____

____

____

____

***Don't forget: Listen** to your Financial Abundance Audio today.*

DAY 40–THE ENERGY OF JOY

Prompt:

If joy were your compass today, what would you choose? What shifted?

Mantra for the Day:

> *Joy is my guide, and it leads me straight to abundance.*

Inspiration:

Clients shared:

"I'd spend time connecting for referrals and stop worrying about social media."

"Joy guided me to find the right attorney for my business—it felt aligned."

Now it's your turn. If joy were your compass, what would you choose today?

____

____

____

____

____

____

____

Don't forget: Listen to your Financial Abundance Audio today.

DAY 41–THE ENERGY OF FAITH

Activation:

Declare out loud: "I'm open to magic…" and then finish the sentence with something unexpected that could bring money, joy, or opportunity into your life.

Mantra for the Day:

I am open to the magic of abundance in all forms.

Inspiration:

Clients shared:
  "I'm open to a new high-ticket client landing in my lap."
  "I am open to an interview with a national publication."
  "I'm open to a client resonating with my post and reaching out."
  Now it's your turn. What magic are you open to today?

____

____

____

____

____

____

____

Don't forget: Listen to your Financial Abundance Audio today.

DAY 42—THE ENERGY OF JOY

Prompt:

Name 10 things you love about your week ahead.

Mantra for the Day:

Joy is my compass, and I follow it with ease.

Inspiration:

Clients shared:

"Vacation, play with kids, sunrises, running, seafood, sunsets, paddle boarding, sand, dolphins."

"New gym, dinners with my husband, my pups, writing my book, and building my course."

"Work with my partner, evenings with my kids, dog walks, bestie lunch, and spontaneous holiday fun."

Now it's your turn. What do you love about your week ahead?

____

____

____

____

____

____

____

Don't forget: Listen to your Financial Abundance Audio today.

DAY 43–THE ENERGY OF ENTHUSIASM

Prompt:

Where can you bring more lightness and fun into your day today?

Mantra for the Day:

I infuse my day with lightness, fun, and enthusiasm.

Inspiration:

Clients shared:

"Laughter and play with my kids."
"Using EFT tapping before business emails to send good vibes."
"Evening canoe on the lake, it feeds my soul."
Now it's your turn. How will you add more fun today?

____

____

____

____

____

____

____

____

Don't forget: Listen to your Financial Abundance Audio today.

DAY 44–THE ENERGY OF EMPOWERMENT

Prompt:

Choose one money belief to let go of and replace it with a new, empowering one.

Mantra for the Day:

I choose to believe in abundance, ease, and possibility.

Inspiration:

Clients shared:

"Old belief: No one is buying. New belief: There are always people who want what I have."

"Old belief: I don't belong with rich people. New belief: I belong everywhere."

"Old belief: Money only comes from activity. New belief: I can make money with balance."

Now it's your turn. What belief will you release and replace?

____

____

____

____

____

____

____

Don't forget: Listen to your Financial Abundance Audio today.

DAY 45–THE ENERGY OF CELEBRATION

Prompt:

Let's celebrate: what have you shifted, learned, or embodied since the start of this journey?

Mantra for the Day:

Every shift I embody makes me more powerful.

Inspiration:

Clients shared:

"I'm more relaxed around money. I broke old family patterns in one session."

"I shifted to serving instead of selling and use EFT to regulate my energy."

Now it's your turn. What's changed for you since the beginning?

____

____

____

____

____

____

____

Don't forget: Listen to your Financial Abundance Audio today.

DAY 46–THE ENERGY OF POSITIVE EXPECTATION

Prompt:

If you could receive one amazing surprise today, what would it be?

Mantra for the Day:

I expect delightful surprises to flow into my life.

Inspiration:

Clients shared:

"A lake house price drops, and my dad's stress is relieved."

"During tapping, I got an email—my stress is over, and abundance is on the way."

"I'm ready to be surprised by a new ideal client."

Now it's your turn. What amazing surprise would you love to receive?

____

____

____

____

____

____

____

Don't forget: Listen to your Financial Abundance Audio today.

DAY 47—THE ENERGY OF EMPOWERMENT

Prompt:

What's one decision you've been putting off that would free up energy? Make it or take the first step today.

Mantra for the Day:

Decisive action frees my energy and welcomes abundance.

Inspiration:

One client shared:

"I'd been dragging my feet on invitations to my retreat. This week I'm creating the video and sending the deposit."

Now it's your turn. What decision will you make today?

____

____

____

____

____

____

____

____

____

Don't forget: Listen to your Financial Abundance Audio today.

DAY 48–THE ENERGY OF TRUST

Activation:

Say aloud:

"Abundance is my natural state."

Don't rush it. Repeat it slowly, again and again, until the words begin to feel true in your body. Notice what happens in your breath, in your posture, in your energy as you keep declaring it.

You were born abundant. Before you ever worked a job, built a business, or made a single decision, abundance is your birthright. Trusting that abundance is your natural state is not about pretending. It's about remembering who you really are.

Mantra for the Day:

Abundance is my natural state.

Now it's your turn. Declare it, repeat it, and let it anchor in.

____

____

____

____

____

____

____

Don't forget: Listen to your Financial Abundance Audio today.

DAY 49 – THE ENERGY OF OPTIMISM

Prompt:

If everything felt aligned, abundant, and easy today, what would be different?

Mantra for the Day:

Optimism opens me to the future I desire.

Inspiration:

One client shared:

"I'd have another retreat signup, two more in my challenge, and I'd be journaling with excitement."

Now it's your turn. What shifts if everything feels aligned and easeful today?

____

____

____

____

____

____

____

____

Don't forget: Listen to your Financial Abundance Audio today.

DAY 50–THE ENERGY OF FREEDOM

Prompt:

What's one thing you can release today (physical, mental, or emotional) to create space for more?

Mantra for the Day:

> *Releasing what no longer serves me creates space for freedom and flow.*

Inspiration:

Clients shared:

"Letting go of a personal battle to create room for love and opportunity."

"Releasing mom guilt about skipping a summer holiday to build my business."

"Letting go of beating myself up for undone to-dos."

Now it's your turn. What will you release today?

____

____

____

____

____

____

Don't forget: Listen to your Financial Abundance Audio today.

DAY 51—THE ENERGY OF TRUST

Prompt:

What would it look like if you fully trusted that money always comes back multiplied?

Mantra for the Day:

Every dollar I spend comes back to me multiplied.

Inspiration:

Clients shared:

"Spending on kids and self-care would feel lighter. I want to feel comfortable."

"Choosing to believe spending on important things creates energy flow that comes back because I feel better."

Now it's your turn. What shifts when you fully trust money always returns multiplied?

____

____

____

____

____

____

____

Don't forget: Listen to your Financial Abundance Audio today.

DAY 52–THE ENERGY OF GRATITUDE

Prompt:

What would it feel like to embody pure gratitude right now?

Mantra for the Day:

> *Gratitude expands everything I touch.*

Inspiration:

Clients shared:

"Journaling gratitude during health challenges made my body feel lighter."

"I started a journal, and deep, rich gratitude is available anytime."

Now it's your turn. Step into gratitude and write what it feels like for you in this moment.

____

____

____

____

____

____

____

____

Don't forget: Listen to your Financial Abundance Audio today.

DAY 53—THE ENERGY OF TRUST

Activation:

Walk through today with unshakable self-trust. Every decision, every action, every conversation, let it come from the belief that everything is working out in your favor. How are you going to trust yourself today?

Mantra for the Day:

I move forward with unshakable trust that everything is working out in my favor.

Inspiration:

Clients shared:

"Going live daily for 21 days leading to my challenge."
"Massive breakthroughs from EFT tapping, trust reinstalled."
"Posted book accolades and signed two more retreat members."
Now it's your turn. How will you walk in self-trust today?

____

____

____

____

____

____

____

Don't forget: Listen to your Financial Abundance Audio today.

DAY 54–THE ENERGY OF JOY

Prompt:

Focus only on joy today. What can you do to bring in joy today?

Mantra for the Day:

Joy is my magnet for abundance.

Inspiration:

Clients shared:

"Creating content for my membership and vision-boarding my lake house."

"Letting go of Friday tennis to create space for travel and joy."

"Finding the right lawyer for my business trademark felt easy and joyful."

Now it's your turn. How will you focus only on joy today?

____

____

____

____

____

____

____

Don't forget: Listen to your Financial Abundance Audio today.

DAY 55—THE ENERGY OF GRATITUDE

Prompt:

How can you end today in gratitude regardless of how it unfolded?

Mantra for the Day:

Gratitude expands everything I touch.

Inspiration:

One client shared:

"I'm grateful for friendship, imperfect action, notes from my kids, and clients who remind me of my purpose."

Now it's your turn. What gratitude are you closing your day with?

____

____

____

____

____

____

____

____

____

Don't forget: Listen to your Financial Abundance Audio today.

DAY 56–THE ENERGY OF CELEBRATION

Prompt:

What are you celebrating about yourself and your journey this week?

Mantra for the Day:

Celebration expands my capacity to receive.

Inspiration:

One client shared:

"I'm celebrating clarity on my new membership, a daily posting streak, excitement for my challenge, and open energy to receive."

Now it's your turn. What are you celebrating about yourself this week?

____

____

____

____

____

____

____

____

Don't forget: Listen to your Financial Abundance Audio today.

DAY 57–THE ENERGY OF OVERFLOW

Prompt:

How can you close out the day in abundance and overflow?

Mantra for the Day:

I end the day grateful and overflowing with abundance.

Inspiration:

Clients shared:

"Facebook group engagement up, book hit bestseller, two retreat enrollments, and long morning snuggles with kids."

"Three new clients, podcast invites, and a trip to Mexico blending business and pleasure."

Now it's your turn. How are you closing out this week in overflow?

____

____

____

____

____

____

____

Don't forget: Listen to your Financial Abundance Audio today.

DAY 58–THE ENERGY OF EXCITEMENT

Prompt:

What are you excited about that's ahead of you?"

Mantra for the Day:

Excitement is magnetic, and I allow it to pull more abundance to me today.

Inspiration:

One client shared:

"I pulled an Oracle card that showed my retreat is a huge success. I'm so excited!"

Now it's your turn. Write about what excites you about the future.

____

____

____

____

____

____

____

____

Don't forget: Listen to your Financial Abundance Audio today.

DAY 59–THE ENERGY OF FUN

Prompt:

How can you bring more lightness, joy, and fun into your day?

Mantra for the Day:

Lightness, joy, and fun bring me more abundance.

Inspiration:

Clients shared:

"A walk for grounding, calling a friend for joy, and playing tennis for fun."

"Daily EFT tapping, music during outreach, and Friday night football with friends."

"Morning ritual, lunch with a bestie, and shopping for a gift."

Now it's your turn. How will you bring lightness, joy, and fun into today?

____

____

____

____

____

____

____

Don't forget: Listen to your Financial Abundance Audio today.

DAY 60—THE ENERGY OF CONFIDENCE

Prompt:

How can you bring confident, unstoppable energy into your day?

Mantra for the Day:

Confidence and bold energy bring me more abundance.

Inspiration:

Clients shared:

"I brought confidence by doing reach-outs, updating my landing page, and posting on social media."

"I felt unstoppable starting my challenge with bold energy."

Now it's your turn. How will you show up with unstoppable confidence today?

Don't forget: Listen to your Financial Abundance Audio today.

DAY 61–THE ENERGY OF POSITIVE EXPECTATION

Prompt:

What wonderful thing are you expecting to happen today?

Mantra for the Day:

Miracles are always on their way to me.

Inspiration:

One client shared:

"I'm welcoming excitement and commitment in my 21-day challenge. I feel a miracle on the rise!"

Now it's your turn. What wonderful thing are you expecting today?

Don't forget: Listen to your Financial Abundance Audio today.

DAY 62–THE ENERGY OF PASSION

Prompt:

What's one thing you can do today that makes you feel lit up?

Mantra for the Day:

When I feel lit up, I attract even more abundance.

Inspiration:

Clients shared:

"I launched a 3-pack of sessions and talked about it live. Clarity feels amazing."

"After a tough call, I ran, called a friend, pulled a card, and treated myself. Now, I'm calling in retreat yesses."

Now it's your turn. What will light you up today?

____

____

____

____

____

____

____

____

Don't forget: Listen to your Financial Abundance Audio today.

DAY 63–THE ENERGY OF BELIEF

Prompt:

How can you see everything today as proof that things are working out?

Mantra for the Day:

Everything is always working out for me!

Inspiration:

One client shared:

"Everything in my life feels like a gift. I can see it, feel it, and I know it's working out for me."

Now it's your turn. How is everything working out for you today?

____

____

____

____

____

____

____

____

Don't forget: Listen to your Financial Abundance Audio today.

DAY 64–THE ENERGY OF CELEBRATION

Prompt:

What's one thing from this week you're most proud of or grateful for?

Mantra for the Day:

> Celebration and gratitude for this week bring me even more abundance.

Inspiration:

One client shared:

"I'm celebrating clarity on my offers, engagement in my challenge, and letting go of fear."

"I'm celebrating a call booked from my email today."

Now it's your turn. What are you proud of or grateful for this week?

____

____

____

____

____

____

____

Don't forget: Listen to your Financial Abundance Audio today.

DAY 65–THE ENERGY OF EXCITEMENT

Prompt:

How can you step into the new week with excitement and joy?

Mantra for the Day:

Excitement and joy bring me more abundance.

Inspiration:

Clients shared:

"I'm motivated and excited—it's bringing health-focused people into my world."

"The portal for abundance stayed open. An old LinkedIn contact circled back with an exciting opportunity."

Now it's your turn. How will you step into this week with excitement and joy?

____

____

____

____

____

____

____

Don't forget: Listen to your Financial Abundance Audio today.

DAY 66–THE ENERGY OF EMPOWERMENT

Prompt:

If you were to brag about yourself today, what would you say?

Mantra for the Day:

Celebrating myself brings even more abundance my way.

Inspiration:

Clients shared:

"I'm proud of the service I'm providing, enjoying my kids and my body, and basking in my hard work daily."

"I'm great at finding clarity for clients, I love my health and life, and I'm proud of being an amazing mom."

Now it's your turn. What makes you amazing?

____

____

____

____

____

____

____

Don't forget: Listen to your Financial Abundance Audio today.

DAY 67—THE ENERGY OF FAITH

Prompt:

If your higher self spoke to you today, what would she say?

Mantra for the Day:

My higher self always guides me toward more abundance.

Inspiration:

One client shared:

"She would say everything I need is already inside. I'm protected by radiant light, and my heart knows the answers."

Now it's your turn. What would your higher self say to you today?

____

____

____

____

____

____

____

____

Don't forget: Listen to your Financial Abundance Audio today.

DAY 68–THE ENERGY OF GRATITUDE

Prompt:

How can you look at everything today with gratitude and as a blessing?

Mantra for the Day:

Gratitude multiplies my abundance.

Inspiration:

Clients shared:

"I'm grateful for sunshine, clouds, and community—reminders that anything is possible."

"I'm grateful for family health, friendships, clients, and the systems that bring me clarity and focus."

Now it's your turn. What blessings do you see around you today?

____

____

____

____

____

____

____

Don't forget: Listen to your Financial Abundance Audio today.

DAY 69–THE ENERGY OF OPTIMISM

Prompt:

How can you see everything today as a sign that good things are on the way?

Mantra for the Day:

> *Good things are always flowing to me.*

Inspiration:

One client shared:

"A client signed up for my program while I was at tennis, such a clear sign that more good things are coming!"

Now it's your turn. What signs are showing you that good things are on the way?

Don't forget: Listen to your Financial Abundance Audio today.

DAY 70–THE ENERGY OF LOVE

Prompt:

What are three things you absolutely love about yourself and your business?

Mantra for the Day:

Loving myself and my business brings me more abundance.

Inspiration:

One client shared:

"I love my authenticity, I love how my business flows with ease, and I love the balance I've created between home and work."

Now it's your turn. What do you love most about yourself and your business?

____

____

____

____

____

____

____

Don't forget: Listen to your Financial Abundance Audio today.

conclusion

Dear Abundant B,

I am so proud of you for getting here. You made it to the end of this book, which tells me something powerful about you. You are ready to rise. You've read, reflected, maybe tapped along, written in your journal, or even created your own Financial Abundance Audio. Perhaps you've completed the 70-day Money Manifestation Activation and started to notice magic unfolding in your world, money showing up in unexpected ways, new opportunities, a calm confidence replacing worry, and a softness in your relationship with money.

And maybe, just maybe, the tangible abundance hasn't arrived yet. If that's you, please don't despair. Abundance isn't a one-time event. It's a frequency, a practice, a relationship you get to keep returning to and keep improving. Every time you shift a thought, soften a fear, or choose gratitude instead of doubt or worry, you are realigning with that frequency. The more you practice, the more natural it becomes.

Even if nothing looks different yet (though I find that hard to believe), can you feel the difference? Doesn't it feel better to live in this energy, and feel open, hopeful, connected, and inspired? Imagine if the entire world operated from this vibration. What a beautiful and amazing place it would be.

This is why I love my Money Mindset and Manifestation Accelerator. It's a whole group of women who want to practice and be reminded daily of staying in this positive energy. It's a space where we don't have to explain why we believe in miracles or why we talk about energy as easily as we talk about strategy. We just get it. We lift each other, we celebrate with each other, and we magnetize more abundance together naturally.

There was a time in my own journey when I thought abundance meant a number in my bank account. I believed that once I hit a certain income level, the anxiety would fade and the freedom would come. But after building a multi-six-figure business, I still found myself holding my breath, afraid to spend, afraid to slow down, afraid to trust.

I knew the numbers. I could create a spreadsheet for any situation. But what I couldn't spreadsheet away was the fear that no matter how well I did, it might all fall apart tomorrow. I was living in "what if" energy: what if a client left, what if sales slowed down, what if this didn't last?

It wasn't until I began not just doing this inner work, but really living it too—the mindset shifts, the tapping, the surrendering—that everything truly changed. I stopped forcing and started allowing.

I stopped trying to control the "how" and began trusting the "when."

I let go of the anxiety and hustle and embraced the peace and surrender.

There was a moment, right after I let go of all my CFO retainers, when I felt like I was standing on the edge of a cliff. The logical part of me was terrified. But the intuitive part, the part I had ignored for so long, whispered, "Leap, and the net will appear." So I leapt.

And the net appeared. Clients showed up in ways I never could have planned. Opportunities expanded. I found myself in complete alignment with the work I love. What I've noticed since living in this energy is how powerfully it radiates outward. I never get tired of hearing, "I love your energy." I love how it feels in my body, how it lights up my life, and how it naturally brings happiness, peace, and ease into everything I do. I've realized abundance isn't something I needed to get. It was something I could become.

When I finally embodied that truth, the outer world began to mirror it back. Money flowed in more consistently. My confidence grew. Life felt lighter. And for the first time in my adult life, I felt peace, real, deep, grounded peace.

That's what I want for you. Not just more money (though that's wonderful too), but more joy, more ease, more connection, and more trust in the beautiful unfolding of your life.

Remember, something extraordinary happens when women gather with shared intention. Our energy amplifies. Our manifestations accelerate. We understand that we were never meant to do this alone. There's a saying that you are the average of the five people you spend the most time with. The same is true for your energy. When you surround yourself with women who are expanding, growing, believing, and receiving, you rise with them.

Whether you join me inside my community or find your own community of like-minded women, please don't isolate yourself on this journey. Surround yourself with people who speak the language of abundance, who will remind you of your power when you forget, and who will celebrate the miracles that unfold as you rise. We always rise faster when we rise together.

The work doesn't end here. This is just the beginning of your abundant evolution. Keep tapping. Keep visualizing. Keep choosing thoughts that feel good. Keep tracking your wins, no matter how small. And when doubt creeps in (because it will), return to the practices in this book. Remember, you can't do this wrong. Every small act of awareness, every shift toward gratitude or trust, ripples out into the universe in ways you can't yet see.

There will be days when you feel fully connected and radiant, when the money flows, the ideas spark, and everything seems effortless. And there will be days when you feel like nothing is working. On those days, your only job is to come back to your energy. Pause, breathe, maybe listen to a visualization or do a little tapping. And remember who you are…an Abundant B.

If you want, pause for a moment right now. Close your eyes and picture yourself one year from today. You're smiling, grounded, and glowing with confidence. You've released the old fears around money and fully stepped into your power as an Abundant B. You trust the flow. You honor your worth. You're surrounded by people and opportunities that reflect the frequency of abundance you've become.

Take a deep breath and feel that vision in your body. That version of you is already real, and she's cheering you on (and so am I).

Abundant B Mantra:

I am open. I am worthy. I am an Abundant B.

Say it often. Write it on your mirror. A post-it note on your computer. Speak it into your morning coffee. Because you are.

As you move forward, remember that you are part of something bigger, a movement of women who are rewriting the story of abundance, wealth, and worth. I would love to continue this journey with you. Come find me on Instagram or Facebook at

@TheManifestingCFO. Share your wins, your stories, and your magic. Tag me so I can celebrate with you, because your success is a reflection of the energy we're co-creating together.

So go out there and live it. Shine, serve, and receive. And remember, the universe is always conspiring in your favor.

With love and infinite abundance.

Xoxo,

Audrey Faust

The Manifesting CFOTM

P.S. I'll be here cheering you on all along the way!

about the author

Audrey Faust, MBA, is a world-renowned thought leader on financial empowerment for women entrepreneurs and the creator of The Manifesting CFO™ brand. Known for blending the power of mindset, energy, and financial strategy, Audrey helps women manifest, manage, and multiply money with ease and confidence.

Through her bestselling book *She Grows Rich: How to Become a Financial Powerhouse*, her signature Profitable Business Academy course, her transformative Money Mindset & Manifestation Accelerator community, and her in-person and online speaking events, Audrey empowers women to master their finances, rewire their beliefs, and create businesses that thrive in both profit and purpose.

A Certified NeuroCoach and EFT Practitioner, she combines brain-based tools, energy work, and CFO-level strategy to help women embody abundance and make confident, aligned financial decisions.

As a self-made multi-millionaire who built her first business from the ground up and helped companies scale to multi–seven figures using her proven CFO strategies — with clients even attaining eight-figure exits — Audrey knows firsthand what it takes to turn financial struggle into sustainable success. Her mission is to help women around the world build wealth, freedom, and confidence while rewriting the rules of what's possible for their lives and businesses.

Audrey lives the snowbird life, spending six months in Naples, Florida, and six months near her children and grandchildren outside of Philadelphia, Pennsylvania.

Connect with her on Facebook and Instagram @ManifestingCFO.